FOCUS ON

LAKE MERRITT

Essays on a unique, urban, natural resource in Oakland, CA

Essays One – Seventy Seven
1991 – 1997

A Year in the Life of Lake Merritt
2002

Photographs by John Kirkmire

Essay Seventy Eight: The Journey Continues
2024

Published by TERRA Productions

ISBN   978-0-9890592-2-0

Cover photo by Lee Aurich
http://www.aurich.com/photos/index.html

Text photos by John Kirkmire
https://www.nowandlens.com/

DEDICATED TO

My wife Susan, who makes the world a better place

Everyone who has volunteered at Lake Merritt

Water, which supports all life, and soothes our souls

TABLE OF CONTENTS

Introduction

Map of Lake Merritt

Essays

Interlude

A Year in the Life of Lake Merritt

Photos of Lake Merritt by John Kirkmire

Epilogue

Essay 78

The Journey Continues by Jonathan Hoffberg

Citations to Previous Management Plans and Studies

About the author

INTRODUCTION

What was Lake Merritt like in the 1990's? Is history repeating itself?

Between September 3, 1991 and December 19, 1997, the Montclarion newspaper (now part of the Bay Area News Group) published a series of 77 essays written bimonthly by Dr. Richard Bailey, founder of the Lake Merritt Institute. These stories, editorials, fantasies, and news briefs, were mostly written in an Irish pub, and provided support for establishment of the Lake Merritt Institute in 1992, Measure DD (The Oakland Trust for Clean Water and Safe Parks) in 2002, and many of the improvements that citizens and wildlife now enjoy around the lake.

Early essays dealt with singular topics such as fountains, birds, and algae. Later essays delved into philosophical issues such as religion, the devil, and ethics. Some concerned economics, history, and the future. Although most had photographs, these have been omitted here in a quest for simplicity and frugality.

During these years, the Lake Merritt estuary was subject to seasonal blooms of algae that reached nuisance levels, as well as plankton blooms and recurrent episodes of very low oxygen in certain areas such as the mouths of storm drains and elsewhere. Initially, herbicide was used to control algal growth, followed by experimental algal pumping, and eventually harvesting. Extensive growths of widgeon grass were also observed in the spring, and harvested. Later, they all but disappeared. The Lake Merritt Resource Enhancement plan was funded, written, and partially implemented. City council members came and went. Intermittent water quality and bacterial monitoring was conducted. Small, white tubeworms that looked like coral and known then as *Mercierella* and now as *Ficopomatus* were common, then almost disappeared. A mermaid was reported, and plankton were said to be talking. Storm drain filters were installed, polluters pilloried, wetlands proposed, a Fishing in the City program started but then stopped, and annual management reports were published by Alameda County. Aeration fountains were installed, volunteers were recruited and U-Clean-It boxes were built. It was a very busy time at the Lake.

As described in the initial essay by editors at the Montclarion:

> Its purpose will be to educate readers about this natural resource that means so much to Oakland, its water quality, and potential improvement projects. Authored by Dr. Richard L. Bailey, the series was created to be educational, entertaining, and easily understood. The articles will promote improvement of the lake by emphasizing positive attributes, praising worthy programs, and encouraging civic pride and stewardship of the Lake's resources.

These essays have been reprinted here in the hope that they will continue to inspire governments, nonprofits, and citizens to increase efforts to create sustainable, permanent improvements to both infrastructure and maintenance of a unique, urban estuary. Hopefully you will be inspired by what has been done, and will act. The opportunities, some are described in the epilogue and in essay 78, are many.

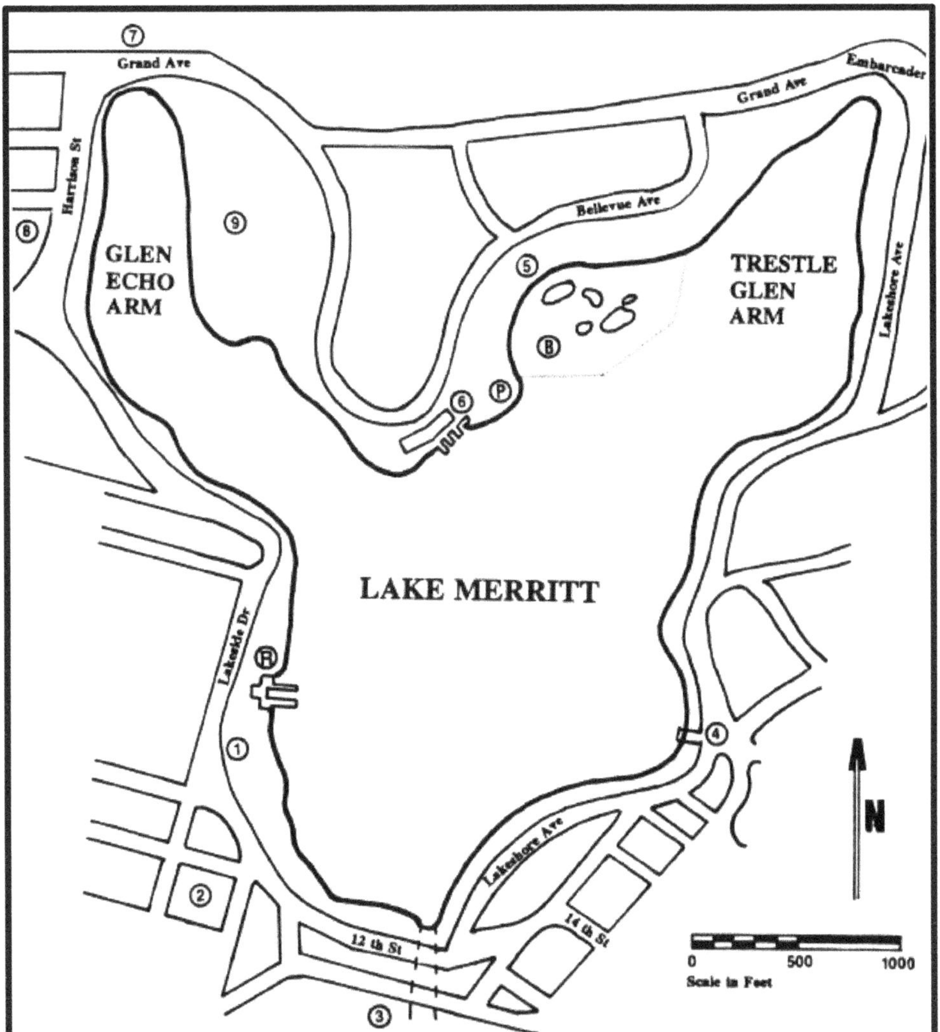
Grand Ave
Harrison St
GLEN ECHO ARM
Grand Ave
Embarcader
Bellevue Ave
TRESTLE GLEN ARM
Lakeshore Ave
LAKE MERRITT
Lakeside Dr
Lakeshore Ave
12 th St
14 th St
N
0
500
1000
Scale in Feet

LAKE MERRITT RESOURCE ENHANCEMENT PLAN
WATER QUALITY ASSOCIATES

LEGEND:

1 Camron Stanford House
2 Courthouse
3 Convention Center
4 18 th St. Outfall Structure
5 Rotary Science Center
6 Sailboat House
7 Veterans Memorial
8 Kaiser Building
9 Childrens Fairyland
B Bird Refuge
P Parking Lot
R Rowboat House

ESSAYS

September 3, 1991 – December 19, 1997

1. LAKE MERRITT: A RESOURCE TO TREASURE

September 3, 1991

What is Lake Merritt? "A lake," says one citizen. "No! A tidal estuary," says another. "An *urban* estuary" says a third. "The Jewel of Oakland," says the Tribune. " A wildlife refuge, America's first," states a student. "It's my home," gurgles the Lake Merritt Mermaid (yes, she really is out there). Other answers might include "a big pond, sometimes smelly" or "my jogging path." "The view from my office/home window" would apply to some of us, and "the peace and quiet that calms my soul" could be said by many more.

To the city's Office of Parks and Recreation, it is home to Lakeside Park, which in turn supports Children's Fairyland, the Lake Merritt Breakfast Club, Garden Center, Boathouse, Junior Cener of Art and Science, and Rotary Science Center. Would these facilities have been brought into existence without the Lake?

In reality, the Lake has profoundly influenced the land around it, from skyscrapers to parks, from homes to public buildings. One wonders how much Lake Merritt contributes to real estate values in Oakland, or to the hundreds of migratory waterfowl that fly in from the arctic every winter.

Such is the obvious relationship of the resource to the city. But isn't there more? Is there a deeper benefit of the body of water that Dr. Samuel Merrit began to create 100 years ago? What would the land use be in this area of Oakland without the Lake?

What is the value of enjoyment that people obtain from the Lake, or the relaxation and long range views that allow them to forget problems and restore their perspective? And what would the joggers, boaters, sightseers, and waterfowl watchers do if the Lake wasn't there?

Truly, Lake Merritt has an influence on people, and a positive one at that. Aesthetically and spiritually, personally and as a city, the resource is a source of pride, hope and inspiration. If I were a literary eccentric, I would say it is part of the "there" in Oakland.

2. SHARKS DISCOVERED IN SURVEY OF LAKE MERRITT

September 13, 1991

Sharks, in Lake Merritt? Yes, but not the man-eating kind. In both of two recent fish surveys conducted at the Lake, specimens of small, common Bay Area sharks were discovered. During January of 1990, two leopard sharks about 28 inches long were captured, and in September of 1990, four brown smooth-hound sharks about 22 inches long were found.

Given the small size and docile nature of these fish, they are not considered dangerous. Leopard sharks are generally timid around divers, and brown smooth-hounds seldom grow larger than three feet long. They are, however, a part of the diverse variety of life beneath the waters that thousands of people jog around every day.

Whether these creatures are a permanent part of the Lake Merritt estuary, or were just visiting is currently unknown. Openings at the bottom of trash racks on pumps that control the Lake's water level are about eight inches wide, ample for the passage of such large fish.

The gray, black and white (spotted like a leopard) shark is known to be nomadic, moving into an area for a short time, then departing. The fact that the brown smooth-hounds were found in the fall, but not in winter when rains lower the salinity levels, may indicate that these fish use Oakland's urban estuary on a seasonal basis. Further research such as mark and recapture studies would supply answers to such questions.

Both types of shark feast on the many types of crabs, shrimps and small fishes that call Lake Merritt home. Their presence in our city waters indicates the recent improvements in water quality and the restoration of the estuary have been beneficial not only to aesthetic values, real estate, and civic pride, but also to the fish and wildlife that share the Lake with us.

Next: "Day of the Algae" will focus on what happens in Lake Merritt when planktonic algal blooms take over the water!

3. ALGAE BLOOMS ON LAKE MERRITT

September 20, 1991

There was a curious, reddish color to the water that day. It shimmered across the Trestle Glen arm of Lake Merritt, not its usual blue color under the clear, late summer sky. Beneath the surface, red algae were at work producing massive quantities of dissolved oxygen which spread throughout the water.

An algae bloom was occurring: Not the usual green type of algae that infest the shallow shoreline, but a bloom of tiny, one celled organisms called dinoflagellates. Such blooms are common in estuaries, and their occurrence does not mean that the water is polluted. But for fish and other critters, it is an event.

As the bloom spread, oxygen levels continued to rise. Normally, dissolved oxygen will comprise 5 – 9 parts per million of the water, which like the twenty percent oxygen that we breath in the air, is ample for aquatic life. But when an algal bloom hits, supersaturation occurs.

This means that the other life forms in the lake are breathing oxygen at several times the concentration to which they are accustomed.

On this August day in 1990, measured levels rose to forty parts per million, about five times the normal level.

No one saw how the fish, shrimp, and zooplankton reacted that day, but we might speculate based on how breathing such concentrations of oxygen affects people.

Assuming they didn't avoid the bloom, fish might have been seen to be zipping around, racing after food like crazed race car drivers. Shipworms and clamworms may have been frantically waving back and forth, energized by the super-abundant oxygen.

Barnacles, mussels, mud crabs and shrimp could have come out of their shells and burrows to dance, wiggle and cavort. Sadly, we'll never know what happened under the water that day, but next August it will probably happen again.

Next: "Why Not a Fountain" will examine the possibilities of installing a fountain in Embarcadero cove.

Note: Algae, and plankton, are also addressed in essays 12, 20, 26, and 74.

4. OUR LAKE NEEDS A FOUNTAIN

September 27, 1990

Have you ever noticed a faint, sulfurous odor near the Embarcadero area at the end of the Trestle Glen arm of the Lake? Or have you ever seen the bubbles coming up from the sediment there on a hot, calm day? This smelly gas, which probably includes methane and hydrogen sulfide, is produced by the decomposition of leaves, trash and other material carried into Lake Merrit by storm drains. Swept from the streets by rainfall, this "urban runoff" comprises the single largest pollution problem in our urban estuary.

At the Embarcadero, the most visible repercussions from the accumulation of storm drain sediment and pollutants are the shallowness of the water, odors, algal blooms and floating trash.

But there is a hidden, unseen problem. The rotting organic matter uses up oxygen in the water. At times this creates serious oxygen deficiencies that cause stress for fish, kill invertebrates, and increase the odor problems.

At the lake bottom near the petro-barrier (the white, floating boom that extends across the water), oxygen levels of lower than one part per million of water have been measured. Water quality standards to protect aquatic life call for no less than 5 parts per million, making it obvious that we have an oxygen problem at the Embarcadero area of Lake Merritt. The question is, what can be done about it?

In addition to periodic removal of the pollutants, diverting storm water to a treatment site, or reducing the source of the material (topics for future articles) one solution is an aeration device to increase oxygen levels in the water.

Basic planning for such a device will be conducted under a study funded by the California Coastal Conservancy and the City of Oakland.

In addition to estimating oxygen transfer rates and the aerial extent of relief that could be provided, the study should consider aesthetic features, including beautiful fountains that spray water high into the air or in patterns that complement the architectural design of the columns and curving shoreline.

Amenities such as lighting to enhance the visual impact of the spray at night should also be evaluated. If proven feasible and accepted by the city, the next step will be to raise funds necessary for both construction and maintenance of the fountain/aeration device.

It will be expensive, but the next time you pass by this area of Lake Merritt, visualize a spray of water, and the improved oxygen conditions.

5. THE LAKES' WINTER BIRDS

October 4, 1991

A botany teacher of mine once passed a book around class, and written into it was this poem attributed to Frederick Petersen – "Wild Geese."

> They know the tundra of Siberian coasts, and tropic marshes by the Indian Sea,
>
> They know the clouds and night, and starry hosts, from Crux to Pleiades.

Such words create vision of migrating ducks and geese, flying high in the dark sky under blazing stars, winging hundreds of miles on their annual migrations.

My father used to awaken the middle of the night upon hearing flocks of them pass over Chicago, long before the lights, heat and who knows what else made the birds detour around the city.

In Oakland however, they don't detour. They land at Lake Merritt.

Despite the total destruction of the marshes that formerly occupied the lake, hundreds of migratory waterflow still arrive at Lakeside Park every winter.

Packed into their small bodies are enough fat to fly nonstop for hours, a guidance system with pinpoint accuracy, and insulation to withstand icy cold waters and frigid air – quite a marvel of natural engineering.

Sometimes the birds seem skittish, afraid of people and the noise. This is understandable, especially if you consider that the bird may have been born in the Canadian arctic last spring and never seen a person, car or building until it flew into Lake Merritt one night and woke up in a big city.

To better accommodate them, the city extends a boating barrier across the Trestle Glen arm each winter, giving them a little space for themselves.

What brings them to Oakland? Perhaps it's the natural food still grows in our estuary-lake, or the rations of fish and grain from park attendants.

More likely it the data encoded in their genes through the centuries, and passed on by thousands of generations.

Whatever it is, they will soon be here, as they have been for eons, and will continue to be as long as we preserve the natural features of the lake.

6. LAKE MERMAID MAY BE BACK

October 11, 1991

We all know of the Downtown Mermaid, a beautiful statue watching us from her pedestal in the City Center waterway. She is a recent addition to this maritime city, but not the only mermaid in Oakland.

Another has been seen at Jack London Square, passing out golden coins while sitting on a half shell. This one, however, didn't go near the water. But there is a history, supported by recent sightings, of a real mermaid in Oakland.

Long ago and not so far away, ancient Oakland settlers reported seeing a strange sight on the waters of lake Merritt. Some described it as a Loch Ness Monster-type apparition.

Local biologists, however, quickly dismissed that idea. Lake Merrit is too shallow (11 feet or less, depending on the tides) to support such a beast. But the sightings persisted, and the fleeting form gradually became recognized as – the Lake Merritt Mermaid.

Sadly, this beautiful woman was seen less and less often as Oakland developed, until at last she disappeared. And who can blame her? In the 1880's, the vast majority of the city's sewage was dumped into the arms of the Lake, untreated.

There weren't as many people in Oakland then, and the tides (as they do today) flushed the estuary twice daily. But as our numbers grew, so did the problem. Water quality conditions were described as notoriously bad in 1926, and fish kills were reported in 1939.

Hard at work though, were the public works people, building sewers and wastewater treatment facilities. The most recent of these projects, the East Bay Infiltration/Inflow Correction program, continues today.

The efforts of these planners and engineers have been rewarding, as through the years – especially during the 1980's – good water quality began to return to Lake Merritt.

Today, bacterial counts in the center of the lake during the summer are dramatically lower than in years past, and hundreds of topsmelt, yellow-fin gobies, staghorn sculpin and shiner surfperch can be seen in the shallow, near shore waters.

But something else has also been seen. As the waters of the estuary have become cleaner, occasional reports of a large tail, or a large fish with green hair and big, blue eyes have been heard at the Lake Merritt Boathouse and Rotary Science Center.

Some astonished joggers even claim that they have seen a mermaid in Lake Merritt. Has she come back? Will she remain? The answer will depend on our continuing efforts in cleaning the estuary and our commitment to have a home suitable for a mermaid.

7. LAKE IS FATAL TO MOST TURTLES

October 18, 1991

You can see them at the Embarcadero area near the end of the Trestle Glen arm, struggling in vain to find more fresh water to keep them from dying. They are not sea turtles (most of which live in warmer, more tropical waters) but common, fresh water turtles.

Released by persons unknown (apparently as part of a traditional ceremony honoring ancestors) these fresh water creatures cannot live in the salty waters of Lake Merritt. Yet they are often there, sometimes several of them. Others appear at the mouth of what was Glen Echo creek where the concrete channel empties into the lake. Most are seven to twelve inches long, about the size that would be sold in markets for food.

It is a common misconception, perhaps enhanced by use of the word "lake" that Oakland's estuary is a body of fresh water. It is not, and fresh water organisms such as turtles cannot, and do not, long survive when mistakenly released in Lake Merritt.

Twice daily tides sweep in from the Oakland Inner Harbor and San Francisco Bay, carrying waters almost as salty as sea water. Only in the winter when rain and urban runoff dilute the salt does the lake become brackish, intermediate between fresh and sea water.

Had the fresh water streams draining into the Lake not been placed underground in storm drains for flood control purposes, the turtles could move up into the hills, away from tidal influence. It is doubtful however, that these reptiles can make the long, dark journey through the pipes, most of which are dry during the summer except for lawn runoff and similar sources of water.

So, they cling to the rocky bulkheads, near where intermittent fresh water from the storm drains floats above the denser seawater. Many are rescued by city Clean Up Crew that removes trash daily with their long nets. These are taken to the Rotary Science Center, which tries to find appropriate homes for them.

Others, however, do not survive, their kidneys unable to cope with the high levels of salt.

Traditions, especially those honoring ancestors, should be encouraged. But when they mistakenly result in the deaths of the animals meant to honor the dead, one would think that the reasons for the ceremony are compromised.

8. DRAINS BRING TRASH TO THE LAKE

October 29, 1991

Storm drains are pipes that carry rainfall from the streets, not to a water treatment plant, but to a nearby stream, the San Francisco Bay or, in several Oakland watersheds, to Lake Merritt. Dozens of them flow into our urban estuary, carrying not only water but everything that ends up on the sidewalks, streets, parking lots, lawns, and rooftops.

The largest is the Glen Echo channel at Grand and Harrison, and the next in size is eight feet across, entering the Lake at the El Embarcadero area of the Trestle Glen arm.

Another, at the end of 21st St. at Harrison, is six feet in diameter. Three others, 4.5 to 5 feet across also disgorge their pollutant loads at the upper ends of the arms. The remainder are smaller, mostly one to 3 foot pipes that flow into Lake Merrit at numerous points all around the shoreline.

Why are they a problem? Because they carry used motor oil and antifreeze, car wash detergents, eroded soil, trash, pet feces, fertilizer, pesticides, leaves, plastics, and chemicals that are hard to pronounce into our lake.

After the storm of March 2, 1991, over 100 oranges were seen floating behind the floating boom at the Embarcadero! Melons, limes, and other produce could also be identified, as could Styrofoam cups from almost every brand of fast food restaurant in downtown Oakland. Shop owners that sell these cups and people that toss them in the street, take note: they don't look as good when floating in the lake.

The recent cleanup campaign for litter control by the Lake Shore Merchants Association should be given credit for also keeping Lake Merritt clean.

That litter control is not often associated with keeping our waters clean points out an important fact. <u>Most folks don't know that storm drains go to streams, the bay, and Lake Merritt</u>. An educational campaign will soon address this point.

But it's not just trash. At the end of the 22ⁿᵈ St. outfall, sediments smell of sewage, and an oily material is present. In the El Embarcadero area, offshore of 18ᵗʰ St., and beyond the pipe at the Harrison/Lakeside intersection, the sediments all emit hydrogen sulfide gas when disturbed.

Storm drain sediments at the ends of both arms use up oxygen, causing violations of water quality standards. A program to address the urban runoff problem is beginning. Hopefully, it will address the unique and obvious effects of storm drains on Lake Merritt.

The "Jewel of Oakland" is too valuable to allow such pollution to continue unabated.

9. STUDY ON LAKE MERRITT CAN BE A VALUABLE TOOL

November 5, 1991

A local newspaper article published earlier this year described plans for a new study to determine ways to enhance Lake Merritt. Included in the work are to be a determination of the feasibility for restoring a tiny portion of the wildlife refuge as a wetland, an evaluation of methods to alleviate low oxygen conditions at the El Embarcadero area, testing of bottom sediments that need to be dredged, and evaluation of new, non-toxic method of algae control.

Surprisingly, the news was greeted with skepticism in some corners. "Another study: Just what we don't need" was a reaction generated by some people, who apparently would rather see action now to clean up the waters, rather than other document that could sit unused on a shelf. But have the past studies sat unused? I think not. True, all the proposed methods that have been advocated over the years have not been implemented at Lake Merritt; nor should they have been implemented. Covering the entire shoreline with rocks for algal control was considered and rejected, as was closing the tide gates, and installing aeration pipes on the bottom of the whole lake.

Some solutions are too expensive, technically unworkable, politically unacceptable, or some combination of the three. In reality, many of the studies have led to action, and Lake Merritt has improved dramatically because the time was taken to plan out what would work, why, and how. The most recent and dramatic improvement came from a document published in 1982, which led to dredging the estuary, improving water quality, and eliminating most of the nuisance plant growth that choked almost the entire lake in June and July.

That study did not sit on the shelf, and still contains valuable information useful today for those willing to read it. In 1966, a detailed document on flood control was produced which led to construction of the flood gates and elimination of flooding in downtown and nearby areas. Most recently, studies on various methods of controlling algae have eliminated the nuisance aspect of the filamentous growths that formerly choked and smelled up our shoreline.

Far from being a waste of money, past Lake Merritt studies have focused resources on specific problems, and in many cases solved them. The pace of such improvement is slow however. Perhaps it is the delays that generate the cries for action without study. A more appropriate course would be to support the necessary planning, evaluate the recommendations, and promote (financially and politically) the improvements that are appropriate for our lake.

10. THE FIRE AND LAKE MERRITT

November 8, 1991

With many major catastrophes, the full impact becomes known to us only long after the original event occurred. Because the horrible fire that devasted the hills of Oakland happened in an area uphill of Lake Merritt, there may be eventual consequences for the lake.

Some of the storm drains, which long ago replaced most of the natural streams draining from the hills, lead to Lake Merritt. Ashes, chemicals, and whatever else remains in the burned area can be expected to wash into the storm drains and eventually enter the estuary.

How much material is mobilized in that manner, and when it will move, cannot be known. These answers depend not only upon the success of cleanup crews working to clean the streets and the "traps" below the storm drain inlets, but also the timing and severity of rainfall.

Because of the City's rapid cleanup response to prevent flooding from clogged drains, and because our first rain was not a gully washer, there is reason for optimism. After the recent rain, crews that clean the lake did not notice any ash or evidence of the fire.

If future rainfall is well spaced and not severe, soil saturation will not occur for many weeks or months, providing time to prepare and clean the area. The current seeding operation, ash removal and other efforts to keep the storm drains clean will also keep Lake Merrit clean.

These same storm drains that protect us from floods and deliver runoff to the lake may have provided an unexpected benefit. Miraculously, many cats and other animals were found to be alive in areas of almost total destruction. One wonders if they sought shelter underground in cool, damp storm drains. Such instinctive behavior is certainly possible, a throwback to more primitive times when burrows were more common than storm drains.

Despite optimum conditions, we may expect some fire-related material to eventually be washed into the lake. Ash and sediment are likely to be observed after the first big rainfall event, but with luck, will not descend upon the lake in quantities large enough to cause significant problems.

As with past sewage spills from pipeline breaks, tidal flushing can be counted upon to cleanse such foreign material within a matter of days – one to two weeks at most. Ash alone, an alkaline material, will probably not be toxic or cause fish kills. Some of the ash received by the lake will be added to the sediment record, and remain there as part of history.

For both the streams and the lake, natural processes are oriented toward renewal. From these, and from the recoveries that have occurred after recent natural disasters, we may find hope. The Toutle River, clogged by ash from the Mount St. Helens eruption, has cleared beautifully within 10 years of the disaster. And, as described in the January, 1989 special issue of Audubon Magazine, the Yellowstone National Park Fire destroyed, but also replenished the land with nutrients and activated millions of seeds that lie dormant until burned.

As with these areas, the Lake Merritt watershed, and its people, will be renewed.

11. CAN WE ESTABLISH A HEALTHY HABITAT?

November 19, 1991

The Random House College Dictionary defines habitat as "the native environment of an animal or plant." In *Fundamentals of Ecology* by Eugen Odum, habitat is defined as the place where an organism lives, or the place one would go to find it. J. Bailey in *Principles of Wildlife Management* defined habitat as "the kind of biotic community, or set of biotic communities, in which an animal or population lives."

What are the habitats of Lake Merritt, and how well do they fulfill the needs of the plants and animals that live there? To be adequate, habitats must provide all the needs of an organism. These include food, cover, nesting areas, and many other requirements specific to the needs of each species. As a wildlife refuge (America's first), lake Merritt and its parkland should provide a variety of good habitats for the fish, wildlife and plants that are dependent upon us for their existence.

But the refuge was established over 100 years ago and to misquote Bob Dylan, the times, they have been a' changing. Gone are the marshlands that existed when the status of "wildlife refuge" was awarded to the lake. Gone are the mudflats that must have existed with the salt marshes, and gone are the natural stream channels that flowed into the estuary from the hills.

Modified is the natural lake bottom, dredged to deeper depths except along the shallow shoreline. Also modified has been the natural vegetation above the shoreline, and the connection to San Francisco Bay, the source of our estuarine waters.

As our city grew, the lake changed in response to our needs for flood control, recreation, and the aesthetic desire for open water, grass, and man-made habitat. For the wildlife, there were also improvements. The five islands, some apparently created with dredged material, were built to improve the habitat for waterfowl. Fresh water is piped to the nearest island, and food is offered to the large numbers of ducks, geese, herons, egrets, and cormorants. These features, together with the shallow and deep water habitats, and upland park areas, form the core of the Lake Merritt Wildlife Refuge.

Can this core of habitat be improved? Could we, carefully and by design, evaluate existing habitats and create additional new ones for fish and wildlife without impinging on existing uses? For example, could a small, natural marsh be created, and if so, would animals such as red winged blackbirds, song sparrows and oysters use the new habitat? Could artificial reefs be created to provide shelter for a greater variety of fish? Fish such as the sturgeon, salmon and skates have not been reported from the lake, but if proper habitat were made available, maybe (as in the movie "Field of Dreams") they will come.

If the eucalyptus trees on the refuge islands were gradually replaced with native species, would warblers use them? (Eucalyptus trees are being removed from such natural habitats as Angel Island and Point Reyes Seashore). Can we create small pockets of natural habitat in Lakeside Park for wildlife use and as a teaching tool? Should an area be set aside where widgeon grass is allowed to grow without being cut, or can natural stream channels be restored as is happening in many areas of the East Bay?

The opportunities are there. What is needed are commitment, financing, energy, and decision by the public and city officials. Given these ingredients, Lake Merritt habitats can be not only improved, but also expanded.

12. DEALING WITH THE ALGAE QUESTION

November 26/28, 1991

Not all algae (we speak here of the large leaf kind – not microscopic phytoplankton) is nuisance algae. Indeed, when it grows in moderation and is in locations that do not cause a problem, algae provide food, shelter, and oxygen to other living organisms. A multitude of animals such as fish, waterfowl, shrimp, clams, and crabs that live in Lake Merritt not only derive benefits from algae, but in many cases depend upon it for their livelihood.

Without the growth of sheltering fronds, many more juvenile fish and invertebrates would fall prey to predators. Without algae as food, many life forms would have to seek other sources of sustenance, and might not remain at our urban estuary.

But when it grows excessively, dies, smells, attracts flies, traps trash, and looks terrible, algae becomes a nuisance. Such was the problem at Lake Merritt in years past.

Before dredging occurred in the mid '80's, large areas of Lake Merritt were shallow enough to allow light penetration to the bottom, and therefore support growth of filamentous algae (e.g. *Cladophora* and *Enteromorpha*). During the late spring and summer months during periods of unusually warm weather, growths of this algae were unchecked, and clogged many parts of the lake.

After dredging, all of the lake except a shallow band (about 20 or more feet wide) along the shoreline became too deep to allow such algae to grow. In this shallow area though, the problem persisted until 1988, when (after an exhaustive study of options) a mild herbicide was chosen to periodically limit algae growth. The herbicide, aquazine, is applied five times during the summer at 10% of the recommended dosage. The chemical is allowed to remain in the water for two days, and then flushed out by the tides.

This chemical is also used by the California Department of Fish and Game to control algae in their fish hatchery raceways, and can be purchased in drug stores for home aquarium use. Although it is not a hazardous chemical, potential effects at the lake are monitored to ensure that it is not causing side effects. To date it has been shown that aquazine does not concentrate in the water, sediment, or the organisms (mussels and fish) which have been tested.

The effect on nuisance algae is to temporarily eliminate the growths, which grow back in a matter of weeks. In this manner, the nuisance aspect of the algae is controlled, and the benefits of the algae are not eliminated.

This status quo is tolerable, but not ideal. Each year the herbicide program must be reviewed and approved by the Regional Water Quality Control Board, as well as the City Council. It is expensive. A more appropriate approach would allow selective control of the algae according to location, and thus not be invasive to the wildlife refuge portion of the lake. Ideally, the shallow water habitat, essential to many of our Lake's fish, ducks, geese, and other critters, should remain without causing the nuisance algae problem.

At present, it is likely that an alternative method of algae control will be investigated next summer. If effectiveness, cost, and benefits are appropriate, we may be able to solve the nuisance algae problem without loss of shallow water habitat, or use of chemicals.

Note: Algal pumping was replaced by harvesting using the city harvester. But after it tipped over and was damaged, the city began contracting out the operation, which continues.

13. DUCKS TAKE OVER AS WINTER BEGINS

December 6, 1991

It is a more placid time, when fewer joggers and boats disturb the serene water. Sunsets are more vivid, and the necklace of lights more noticeable as darkness comes sooner. Sparkling reflections light up the surface, enhanced by the evening's glow in the sky and over the lake. Winter is coming to Lake Merritt.

Temperatures drop, and algae ceases to grow along the shallow shoreline shelf. Fewer fish are seen in the shallows, forsaking cooler waters for the deeper parts of the lake or open bay. The juvenile fish that grew there are gone, each species to its particular winter niche. The goslings are grown, and their parents will soon take note of the winter solstice, when increasing day length will begin the next nesting cycle.

Migratory waterfowl return in great numbers although (according to some observers) not as many as once graced this urban estuary. Just how many and what is the variation in numbers is the subject of speculation, and a topic that would be well served by a permanent, weekly waterfowl monitoring program such as exists at Lake Elizabeth in Fremont. Any volunteers?

Rainfall, when it arrives, creates a less saline environment, and brings in leaves, nutrients, and urban runoff. When storms are forecast, the lake level is lowered and the tide gates are closed, thus maintaining the lake's flood storage capacity in the event that runoff coincides with a high tide. This results in a continuous exposure of the shoreline in many areas, and the absence of daily tidal flows in the lake. Although this flood capacity is vital, long period is of low levels can dry out the shoreline, negatively impacting populations of invertebrates. Future studies may attempt to define a better balance between flood control and maintenance of a natural tidal cycle.

Perhaps the most beautiful expression of winter on the lake are the floating Christmas trees and the caroling boat tours. Although there is no apparent written history, the caroling tradition dates back to at least the 1920's, making it one of the oldest organized recreation activities in

Oakland. For many families, it wouldn't be Christmas without the color-ful evening excursions across the waters of Lake Merritt. This year the boats, adorned with Christmas trimmings, will make their voyages from Dec. 6 through Christmas eve.

The "Christmas trees on the Lake" tradition was started by the Oakland Chamber of Commerce which decided on the idea at a meeting in Fresno during mid-summer one year. Mel Wall became the father of the con-cept, and was instrumental in actually installing equipment for the first lighting ceremony.   All of Oakland is served by his work. A large, long cable carries 220 volts of electricity to the lights, which formerly cycled through colors by means of a mechanical switch. Sadly, the switch cor-roded and money has not been available for its replacement. When an anchor line was lost one year and the tree barge moved to another loca-tion, residents howled with complaints that they could no longer see the spectacle on the water from their windows. The tree was restored to its original location.

Winter, Christmas, and the turning of the seasons: What would Oakland be without Lake Merritt to help us enjoy them?

14. KEEPING THE LAKE CLEAN EVERY DAY

December 17, 1991

Have you ever wondered what happens to the multitude of paper cups, plastic, cans, bottles, leaves fruit, tennis balls, Styrofoam, and other trash that washes into Lake Merritt? After each rainfall when a few tenths of an inch or more falls on Oakland, the streets are washed of the pollutants, which are promptly flushed by storm drains into the urban estuary.

If you visit the Lake frequently, or if your window overlooks the shoreline, you probably have seen this debris around the larger storm drains, and elsewhere in the water. But the next day, it is gone; disappeared. Although the daily tides carry bacteria, unseen chemicals, and some trash out of the Lake and into the bay, most of the material is removed by the Clean-Up Crew from District One of Maintenance Services, a division of Oakland's Public Works Department.

Under the supervision of Bob Stevens, the three or more man crew does a heroic job of keeping Lake Merritt clean. Armed with long, extendable nets, boots, shovels and rakes, the crew patrols the entire shoreline daily, removing foreign material from the waters and hauling it off in their truck.

Considering the variety of trash that ends up in storm drains and eventually in the Lake, they could probably tell some interesting stories about their daily work. But after these men pass through the area, the Lake is clean. They also remove some of the nuisance algae that grows along the shoreline during the summer.

Not so long ago, the Lake wasn't as clean. Then, the crew patrolled only a portion of the shoreline each day, and trash not picked up was left to float around, or sink to the bottom. Boaters bumped into floating bottles more frequently. Fish nibbled at plastics and wondered what it was.

Complaints, recommendations in lake management reports, and a desire to minimize this most visible form of pollution led to daily patrols of the entire shoreline, and consolidation of the responsibility into one district.

The outcome has been noticeable, and has resulted in a much cleaner lake, with healthier habitats.

So, a hearty Thank You to the Lake Merritt Clean-Up Crew. Their important work ensures that the most visible portion of storm drain pollutants are promptly removed.

And remember, you can help by keeping sidewalks, parking lots and gutters free of trash. I'm sure they wouldn't mind if we reduced their workload.

Note: In later years, Lake Merritt Institute volunteers took over day to day trash removal.

15. CITY CAN'T AFFORD FLOATING TREE DISPLAY

January 3, 1992

Why is the Lake Merritt mermaid crying? Having recently returned to a much-improved existence (part of the "there" in this city), she has just been told that this may be the last year that the traditional floating Christmas holiday trees will be installed on the lake.

The twinkling reflections of colored lights, for years enjoyed by tens of thousands of people (and at least one mermaid) are an apparent victim of decay and, to an extent, budget problems. Children and mermaids are perplexed: They don't understand such matters.

Having inherited the artificial trees and lights from the Chamber of Commerce last year, the city Office of Parks and Recreation arranged for the floating platforms, the long wire cables, and PG&E connections, and it found a qualified firm for installation, replacement of bulbs and storage.

The equipment however, is in very bad shape. The structural components are worn, the lights are burned out, and the effect of corrosive salt water has taken its toll on the 220-volt cables and electrical connections.

Only last-minute repairs will allow the trees and lights to grace the lake one more time this year, continuing what must be a unique city tradition.

Really, has anyone seen floating, lighted trees at any other major metropolis in the United States? But next holiday season, unless money can be raised for new decorations, the tradition may die.

It doesn't have to be that way. With citizen and corporate support, we can avoid darkness on Lake Merritt. The Office of Parks and Recreation will accept donations to rescue this unique Oakland Christmas tradition.

If enough money is raised to replace the trees, the tradition will continue on during the '90s.

Costs for new trees could run as high as $20,000 although this would depend upon the type of tree or decoration that was chosen. The city is open to comments on the type of on-water decoration that would be most appropriate.

Gifts of equipment, specialized services, storage space, etc. are also welcome and would help insure the continuation of Christmas holiday lights across the water.

To make a tax-deductible donation, contact Samee Roberts at the Oakland Office of Parks & Recreation, 1520 Lakeside Drive, 94612 or call her at 273-3090. The Lake Merritt mermaid needs a Christmas tree, and Oakland needs a Santa. Won't you help out?

Note: The Lake Merritt Institute provided decorated trees on the water, and at the Lake Chalet dock until the program was discontinued.

16. MERRITT'S DILAPIDATED FISHING PIERS

January 10, 1992

They survive like reminders of a past era, when Lake Merritt was fouled by obnoxious blooms of summer algae. They were in the same condition when Lakeside Park was dark, unsafe, and home to drug deals and trash. Somehow in the improvements that have come to the estuary and its park, the fishing piers have been forgotten.

Four piers (not counting the boat docks, 18th Street platform or the concrete extension at El Embarcadero) currently extend out into the shallow shoreline waters. One is located just west of the inlet/outlet by 12th street, and three in the Glen Echo arm (at the end of Madison, across from the Veterans Memorial Building on Grand Avenue, and next to the "beach" by the bandshell). Two of them, however are in a disreputable condition. Deteriorated, unsafe, and disconnected from the shore, they stand like eyesore on an otherwise attractive landscape.

The decay is natural, for tidal salt water will have its way with wood. Burrowing organisms, weather, and the continuous wet-dry cycle cause the timbers to rot and fail. When the structures would no longer safely support people, they were cut off from land by city officials. And since then, nothing else has happened: No restoration, no improvements, and continuing lost opportunities to walk into the magic boundary between land and sea. This is not the kind of thing the Chamber of Commerce or Lake Merritt Breakfast Club would be proud of.

Somehow, standing on a pier does more than bring you closer to the water. Ducks and people are more easily brought together, the pier being sort of a transition between their world and ours. Fish, crabs and other critters are more easily observed, especially since some of them would not be there without the structure which provides cover from marauding birds above, and a firm footing on which to attach in a world of shifting water and mud. One feels more distant from the busy land environment when surrounded on three sides by water, and more a part of the placid lake scene. Reflection, observation, fishing, and feeding the waterfowl – all are enhanced by docks.

So why not restore them? Lack of money, manpower, and time are the three "Raiders of the Last Park" that are so often cited by officials. And in this case, it may be absence of a proactive force that seeks out such lost opportunities and works to redress them. It has been rumored that funds for dock repair are available from a state agency, and this needs to be investigated.

If a commitment can be made, let's go first class with a design and materials built to last, and to complement the shoreline. Benches could be included, with feature to keep sea gulls, and their droppings, off of them. Educational signs, like those at the wildlife refuge, would be another plus. Strollers, joggers, dreamers, and the curious would all benefit. And so would Oakland.

Note: The Lake Merritt Breakfast Club later sponsored renovation of the dock on Lakeside Drive.

17. LAKE MERRITT WATER QUALITY TO UNDERGO MAJOR STUDY

February 18, 1992

A new chapter in the improvement of Lake Merritt will begin this spring. Funded by a $90,000 grant from the Coastal Conservancy, and an additional $10,000 from the Parks and Recreation Department, the Lake Merritt Resource Enhancement Plan – Water Quality Study is scheduled to take place over the next four to nine months.

The work will be conducted by several professionals and consulting firms, each a specialist in the task they have been assigned. Their work is expected to lead to an action report, which will recommend specific projects to be funded for the improvement of Lake Merritt.

Why is this work being done? If you have read this column, and if you are familiar with the water quality problems of Oakland's unique, urban estuary, the answer is obvious. Estuaries are sediment traps, and if left unmanaged, sediment will change the lake. Storm drain pollutants, apathy, misinformation, and ignorance can destroy the natural and human values of the resource.

Lake Merritt is, in large part, a man-made resource, and if it is to continue as the "Jewel of Oakland" it needs monitoring, maintenance and improvement. Although this study will not be a cure all, it will begin to shed light on some potential ways to improve the Lake and its water quality. It will also seek ways to implement the improvements, and will ask your help in doing so.

Among the questions the study seeks to answer are: What is the composition of storm drain deposits that need to be dredged from the Lake? How much of this material should be removed? Given the hydrological requirements of flood control and summer events, can a natural marshland be established to benefit wildlife? Can an easily cleaned catch basin be built to remove storm drain sediments? Should an aeration fountain be installed to eliminate areas of low oxygen? Can an area of eroding shoreline be stabilized? Can the winter water level be modified to allow more tidal action during rainfall without risking as flood? Will a mechanical method of controlling algae work?

Advisory committees, existing organizations concerned with the Lake and its resources, and the Lake Merritt Master Plan Committee will be informed of the goals of the study, and their input will be solicited. From this public information process may spring a new citizen movement for Lake Merritt. If the interest is adequate, perhaps a Lakekeeper position could be established, or a volunteer group to conduct weekly monitoring of waterfowl.

The work that is recommended by the action plan will not begin immediately. Funding, permits from regulatory agencies, and approval by the City Council will each be significant hurdles. Overcoming them will depend upon the will of the people as expressed to decision makers, support for funding, and bulldog persistence to fulfill the regulatory permit requirements.

Is Oakland up to the challenge? Given the past record of improvements, the answer should be yes. The Lake Merritt Resource and the Lake Merritt mermaid are counting on you.

Note: The Resource Enhancement Plan was completed in 1992. https://oaklandlibrary.bibliocommons.com/v2/record/S183C1433953

18. MONITORING THE LAKE'S WATER QUALITY

March 24, 1992

"No swimming," warns the sign at the beach. But why? The water looks clear and fine, even inviting. Is the water unsafe, and if so, why? Just what is unsafe anyway? The answer is determined by the bacterial levels.

Since its creation, Lake Merritt has not been "ye olde swimming hole," and in the early days, there was ample reason to stay out of the water. In past decades, untreated sewage flowed to the Lake; directly at first, then as a result of overflowing sanitary sewage which poured into the storm drains. As late as 1976, a detailed bacterial study of the Lake indicated that sewage overflows through man holes was still a problem.

But by 1981, improvements to Oakland's underground plumbing system had eliminated most of the problem, and as of today, only very heavy rains a few times a year result in a mixture of sanitary sewage and storm water entering the Lake. This material is typically flushed out by the tides within a few days.

Although bacterial sampling of the water had been done monthly during the 1970's, the practice all but stopped by the late 1980's, when bacterial samples were taken sporadically, if at all. Then, in 1989, several samples were taken before and after a break in a sanitary sewer line that contaminated the Lake. The results indicated that pre-break conditions, and water quality several days after the spill, were adequate for body contact recreation in most parts of the Lake. In mid-1990, monthly sampling was initiated in five stations.

By 1992, due to the interest of several biologists who care about the Lake, bacterial sampling has increased to twice a month at 6-7 stations. As a result, we now have a much better picture of bacterial levels in Lake Merritt. Although waterfowl contribute some bacteria to the water, the only sources that cause bacterial levels to exceed moderate body contact criteria are the storm drains.

By contemporary health standards, and with the exception of the limited areas adjacent to the petro-barriers at the upper ends of the Glen Echo and Trestle Glen arms of the Lake, Lake Merritt waters are adequate for some forms of body contact recreation (such as wind surfing) during the non-rainy seasons.

But don't count on it. Limited administrative manpower, fiscal constraints relative to sampling costs, anxiety over liability, and an attitude of "keep the Lake like it is; don't overuse it" combine to keep the "no swimming" signs posted. However, it's nice to know that (except when the storm drains are flowing) our urban estuary is clean enough to get wet in. Boaters really don't have to worry if the splash themselves or fall overboard.

And above all, it's time to realize that Lake Merritt is not polluted. Our efforts to improve it have, and continue to be, successful.

Note: In 2023, three 24/7 water quality monitoring buoys were installed in Lake Merritt. See Lake Merritt Commons on back cover for details.

19. ADDRESSING THE FUTURE OF LAKE MERRITT

April 21, 1992

A warm wind moved unobstructed across the waters of Lake Merritt as the spring light faded into darkness. In the wildlife refuge, mallard ducks slept with heads nestled under wing feathers, and black crowned night herons took flight toward sustenance. All appeared peaceful except for the hurried pedestrians visible on the shoreline.

At the Garden center in Lakeside Park, however, all was not peaceful. City council deliberations included issues that would affect the Lake's water quality, and thereby the plants and animals that depend upon it.

And although Lake Merritt is a treasured resource in Oakland, any group of nine concerned citizens will find something about it upon which to disagree. These disagreements can be resolved, but time is required, and funding, too.

Even when funding is available, it must be justified, thereby requiring more time, energy, and people-power; not to mention an office, creativity, and (most important of all) dedication to what is best for the Lake.

How are these requirements for improving Lake Merritt fulfilled? Traditionally, city and county staff play a role. The two city agencies most directly responsible for the Lake are the Office of Parks and Recreation and the Department of Public Works. At the county level, the Flood Control and Water Conservation District has responsibilities, and interests, in Lake Merritt. In some cases, professional consultants and/or contractors can by brought in to conduct specialized work if funding is available.

Private citizens play a role through advisory committees and other groups. Together, these groups have significantly improved the physical condition of the Lake and its parkland, as well as the public perception and enjoyment of the resource.

But still, problems (and opportunities) cry out to be addressed. Why do we have dilapidated fishing piers? Do we have to tolerate the continued pollution from storm drains? Would you like to see the Rotary Science Center become a first-class educational facility with equipment such as spotting telescopes, interactive computer exhibits, and a continuous flow-through aquarium for observation of underwater life?

The current aquarium looks sad and appears doomed to elimination. Can/should a controlled fishing program be implemented with hatchery steelhead such as is done at Lake Merced in San Francisco? Is funding and the political will available for habitat improvements such as a small wetland, underwater fish reefs, and landscaping selected for people and wildlife? Who will fund water quality improvements?

These, and other questions could be addressed by a Lake Merritt Institute, a nonprofit, public interest foundation designed to support research, education, and capital improvements at the Lake.

Such foundations have already been established at several locations in the United States, and they have raised millions of dollars for restoration and maintenance of facilities such as Lake Merritt.

It could happen here. If you are interested, watch this column for details, and for information on how you can become involved in a natural resource called Lake Merritt.

Note: The Lake Merritt Institute was founded in 1992. See Epilogue for current ways to help Lake Merritt.

20. NON-CHEMICAL PUMP CONTROLS ALGAE

June 30, 1992

It seems to work! The experimental method to remove nuisance algae from Lake Merritt has undergone field trials, and shows promise as an alternative to the current use of herbicide. And since the herbicide will soon be removed from the market, the "algal pumping" method may soon become the best way to prevent the large, somewhat odorous, floating mats of algae that trap trash, attract flies, and contribute to the image of a polluted Lake.

For the last several years excess growths of filamentous algae along the shoreline have been controlled by five applications each summer of Aquazine, a mild, aquatic herbicide. The chemical works, and has controlled the widespread massive growths that used to choke the shallow Lake Merritt shoreline.

Although monitoring of the Lake has shown that the chemical does not accumulate in water, sediment, mussels or fish, use of such a chemical is not the ideal method of algal control in a wildlife refuge. And now, because of a lack of profit, regulatory requirements or whatever, Aquazine will no longer be sold. Although the company that supplies it has enough throughout 1992 and perhaps 1993, it will no longer be available when supplies run out.

Enter "algal pumping," a new, experimental approach in which the floating mats are sucked into a 3 inch diameter pipe, broken up by the pump, and discharged into deeper water where the green material sinks, is carried out of the Lake by outgoing tides, and / or dies.

The process removes bubbles (which cause the algae to float) and allows the stuff to sink into deeper, darker water where conditions are inadequate for its growth. In fact, because the method is carried out during tidal flows, there is less worry about causing oxygen depletion, and costs of holding the Lake at a high level for two days are eliminated. Algae pumping offers other advantages, including the possibility of algal removal at specific locations and allowing natural processes to take place elsewhere (such as in the refuge area). With herbicide, treatment resulted in control throughout the entire Lake, like it or not. With the pumping method, one can concentrate on areas most in need of algal removal. Algal pumping also does not affect other plants in the Lake, such as widgeon grass.

The method is simple and uses standard equipment. Limitations include tides high enough to get the barge into shallow water, and the possible need for more frequent control (this is being investigated).

Research is at work; and the outcome may soon result in continuance of a nuisance algal control, by pumping, and a healthier Lake Merritt.

Note: Algal pumping was replaced by harvesting using the city harvester. But after it tipped over and was damaged, the city began contracting out the operation, which continues.

21. A BEAUTIFUL, AFFORDABLE FOUNTAIN CAN SOLVE LAKE MERITT'S WOES

May 19, 1992

The results are in. Prepared as part of the Lake Merritt Resource Enhancement Plan, the engineering technical memorandum evaluating use of an aeration fountain at the El Embarcadero cove declares the following conclusions:

- Commercially available aeration systems can effectively aerate El Embarcadero Cove (the Trestle Glen arm) for a reasonable cost.
- A standard jet-pump aerator is recommended for El Embarcadero Cove as a cost effective measure for reducing anoxic conditions. A similar system might also be installed at the Glen Echo arm of the Lake.

As discussed in a previous edition of the column (Our Lake Needs a Fountain – September 27, 1991), dissolved oxygen levels near zero and disturbing odors often exist in this area. Despite the city symbol and exhortations for a better Oakland imbedded in concrete at the El Embarcadero columns, the problem persists.

But now there is proposal that can both solve the problem and contribute to civic pride, which is something that can help us get through the difficult times brought on by fire, crime, and violence. An aerator fountain such as evaluated in the Enhancement Plan would be viewed and appreciated by thousands of joggers, strollers, babies in carriages, and senior citizens that use this area daily.

Available models can be adjusted to provide a "rocket, phoenix or sunburst" spray pattern. In addition to improving conditions for fish, waterfowl, crabs and shrimp, the sight and sound of softly falling water will add to the serenity of Lake Merritt in the midst of a bustling city.

Will it happen? If support is strong enough, it will overcome the type of bureaucratic opposition that raises barriers but fails to suggest solutions. Total equipment cost is estimated at $3,247 and annual operation-maintenance costs at $1,180. An optional "fountain glo" lighting system with programmable colors would cost an extra $1,215. Can Oakland come up with $5,642 to solve a water quality problem, enhance Lake Merritt and contribute to the enjoyment of lake users? Is there a benevolent individual or corporation out there willing to help? Perhaps the city would enshrine their name on a bronze plaque as was done with the necklace of lights.

Citizens: If you want a fountain, contact your elected representative or city officials. Lake Merritt Breakfast Club; is this a project for you?

Aeration fountains were eventually installed at four locations, but were removed when changes in water level and siltation prevented their operation.

22. LAKE STUDY RESULTS ARE IN; COUNCIL MUST ACT

December 11, 1992

On January 19, the Lake Merritt Resource Enhancement Plan will be on the agenda for subcommittees of the City Council. After nine months of study, the results are in, and the recommendations are ready. Acceptance by the council could begin the process to implement the improvements, and lead to enhanced wildlife habitat, a healthier environment, and more reason to be proud of where we live.

Highlights of the report include a recommendation to provide support for a public / private partnership with the Lake Merritt Institute, a new, nonprofit advocacy organization, formed to advance education, conduct research, and erect and maintain public works. Also recommended are aeration fountains to alleviate the "zero" oxygen conditions that sometimes occur in areas of the Lake.

These fountains could be dedicated to the memory of the late William Penn Mott, past director of Oakland City Parks, California State Parks, and the National Park Service.

Replacement of herbicide use with algal pumping, creation of a few, small high marsh wetland habitats, removal of accumulated storm drain sediments (some are legally toxic) and 15 other specific suggestions are recommended.

But will the City Council approve the report? Our first lesson becomes "Nothing is certain; and never assume that someone else will regard a natural resource in the same light that you do." There are those that would view wetland creation as fill, and not as wildlife habitat. Perhaps they view the Lake as an aesthetic bath tub, inappropriate for mud and pickleweed.

Will the city accept the challenge of replacing herbicide use with mechanical control? It is often easier to block recommendations and do nothing then to work through any complications that enhancements might entail. Yes, the improvements will require time, money, and people, but so does everything else that we do. If Lake Merritt is to be enhanced, the plan should be supported. Let's hope the City Council approves the document, and instructs staff to work diligently with the neighborhood, government agencies and businesses that care about the environment.

Lake Merritt, its wildlife, and all of us will benefit.

Note: The Resource Enhancement Plan was completed in 1992.

https://oaklandlibrary.bibliocommons.com/v2/record/S183C1433953 and
https://www.my.laketech.com/public-portal/LakeMerritt/

23. FINDING WAYS TO KEEP THE CITY AND LAKE CLEAN

February 23, 1993

It starts with the greasy sandwich wrapper thrown carelessly on the ground. Not far away is an empty plastic motor oil bottle and a paper cup left at the bus stop. By now we are all familiar with such litter, and how it degrades property values. But at it's downhill destination, Lake Merritt, it also degrades water quality, stealing oxygen from the water and contaminating sediments. Washed by the rains into storm drains, street litter in much of Oakland becomes Lake Merritt litter.

Concentrated from a watershed area of 3,960 acres into the 145 acre lake, it bobs on the waves for all to see after each rainstorm of more than one tenth of an inch. If we are to stop this (the most significant cause of pollution in Lake Merritt) the watershed must be kept clean. Our watershed is that area of the city (a large portion of central Oakland and Piedmont) from which water flows into the Lake via runoff and storm drains.

But how can the mass of trash left on the streets, sidewalks and parking lots be kept from getting into the storm drains and from there into the Lake? Volunteer cleanup efforts such as "We Mean Clean" and the recently completed "Lake Merritt Institute Cleanups" certainly help by removing mountains of debris, but cannot solve the continuing problem. Even if such endeavors successfully eliminate all litter from the watershed, the following monthly accumulation would again wash into the Lake. To keep Lake Merritt clean, there must be an accepted, and continuous method of keeping Oakland clean.

A friend who travels in foreign countries recently told me that some places now enforce the litter laws with very expensive fines, like many dollars for dropping a cigarette. Such heavy handed control probably wouldn't work here, and besides, the police are already too busy. There ought to be a better way.

When I was a little boy in Chicago, I read that in Holland and other European countries the shopkeepers would begin each day by cleaning the street in front of their store. It didn't take long, five minutes maybe, plus whatever time they spent talking to a neighbor or potential customers. What a great idea. If each property owner took a few minutes each day to remove trash from his grounds, the problem would be solved. Store managers on Grand, Lakeshore, 19th St., etc. could put their litter in the trash can when it was taken out. Landlords and tenants in residential areas might want to volunteer two minutes a day to keep their sidewalk clean. Fast food restaurants could assign an employee to gather up their "advertising" left by careless customers. The transit authority could be made responsible to keep bus and train stops unpolluted.

But would it work on a voluntary basis? Unfortunately, probably not. In a fast paced society such as ours, the little individual actions that collectively make a big difference too often get left undone. This is where the Oakland City government could play a role. Not as a police presence, but to institutionalize the cleanup; to create and gently enforce, a tradition. How about passing a "Pride in Property act," requiring (under penalty of visits, letters, and annoying $10 fines) that each property owner keep their storm, drain, street, sidewalk, parking lot etc. free of trash?

Fines could be more substantial for continual offenders, and monthly awards for best and worst participant could focus public attention as appropriate. If established properly, one dedicated administrator could run the program, perhaps the same person that now coordinates the periodic trash collection. Relying heavily on media exposure, education and personal visits to commercial areas and targeted sites, such a program would generate "Pride in Property." Decals for participants could notify customers and neighbors that this property is kept clean, and doesn't contribute trash to Lake Merritt.

Because most properties are kept clean, the program could focus on those sites where daily litter is a problem. At the same time, the financial benefits to City government would be substantial in terms of reduced labor to clean the lake, enhanced property values, storm drains that didn't plug up, and less city effort required in street cleaning.

So, how about it? Is Oakland ready for a program of continual litter and storm drain abatement? Oakland is already a cleaner city than San Francisco, and implementation of a "Pride in Property Program" would only enhance our prestige. If you are in favor of such a program, why not contact your city councilmember?

24. CITY LOOKS AT PLAN FOR LAKE MERRITT

March 5, 1993

The City Council has approved a move toward looking at long term plans for maintaining, revitalizing, and expanding Lake Merritt and its park surroundings. On Tuesday the council passed a recommendation by the Cultural Services Committee, whose members approved financial support for the Lake Merritt Institute, a community group that wants to assist the city in developing a Lake Merritt Master Plan, which city officials estimate will cost $400,000.

The council approved some $5,000 in funding for the institute, which would work, along with other community groups, as a partner with the city in overseeing the lake. Two members of the group, Winifred Walsh, and Anne Bruff, said the group's current active program is monitoring some 100 storm drains and two creeks in the lake area.

The group is set to do fundraising for the park and Walsh and Moore called the newly elected City Council's attitude towards the park "visionary." Councilmember Sheila Jordan, who chairs the council's Cultural Services Committee, said that staff will review plans drawn up years ago for a Lake Merritt Park that stretches all the way to Oakland's marina at Jack London Square. Council member Dick Spees said the plans were developed by students at the University of California, but action on them was never taken.

The council's new members said they were interested in seeing the blueprint for a Lake-to-Bay Park, which Spees said was an interesting idea, though expensive.

Note: A Lake Merritt Master Plan was completed in 2002 (https://www.wrtdesign.com/projects/lake-merritt-master-plan).

25. RESTORATION OF WETLANDS MUST BE A PRIORITY

March 9, 1993

They're gone: Destroyed by dredging, filled by bulkheads, and prevented from regrowth by limited tidal flow, the former lake Merritt wetlands now exist only in scattered clumps of gum plant and salt grass. So scattered, in fact, that it took a recent survey by experts to determine that remnants of salt marsh vegetation still exist around the borders of our central, downtown estuary. The survey, and a coordinated study of tidal levels, were part of the Lake Merritt Resource Enhancement Plan. The studies concluded that a high marsh of plants such as pickleweed, salt grass, gum plant, etc. can be established in Lake Merritt.

The enhancement plan, yet to be approved by the Oakland City Council, rates "Create High Salt Marsh Wetland Habitats" as number four in a list of 20 recommendations. Only "Support the Lake Merritt Institute," "Install an aerator fountain," and "Replace Herbicide Use with Algal Pumping" were ranked higher. This high priority was assigned to wetland creation for the following reasons:

- An estuarine wildlife refuge without salt marsh habitat is sad example of our past callous indifference to natural environments. If Lake Merritt were to be evaluated today, the status of "wildlife refuge" that was awarded when its wetlands existed would be difficult to justify.
- The proposed high salt marsh habitats could serve the dual purpose of badly needed erosion control at two of the proposed sites.
- The wetlands would not be monster marshes as feared by a member of the City Council, which appears to equate wetland creation with filling in the Lake. The proposed four areas would range in size from 0.4 to 0.9 acres, for a total of 2.3 acres (1.5 percent of the estuary's surface area).
- They would provide educational value to local students. Why shouldn't Oakland's students be able to find a salt marsh wetland to study in Oakland?

Properly designed and built high salt marsh wetlands would not create mosquito breeding areas, as substantiated in the Enhancement Plan. Being adjacent to shallow shoreline areas, they would not interfere with boating activities. Containment structures to prevent erosion and retain marsh material should be built to remain above the surface at high tide.

Potential locations for wetland restoration are: Two sites around the outer island of the wildlife refuge; east of the inlet / outlet channel where erosion is undercutting the bridge; and below the eroded, steep bank on the southwest side of the Lakeside Park Point. The habitat benefits of such sites were discussed in "Can We Establish a Healthy Habitat?" in the Nov. 19, 1991 issue of the Montclarion.

Wetland restoration is occurring at many sites in San Francisco Bay. But it seems that no other area offers as much opportunity to bond education, wildlife habitat improvement, and erosion control together in one project than does Lake Merritt. Given the thousands of people that enjoy the Lake every day, the public would benefit immensely from wetland restoration at Lake Merritt, as would all of Oakland.

Further information on the potential restoration can be obtained from the Lake Merritt Institute, 1520 Lakeside Drive, Oakland, CA 94612.

Note: Small, high marsh wetlands have been established at the Boating Center parking lot and along the channel. The latter site has been frequently vandalized.

26. NEW ALGAE CONTROL METHOD WILL BENEFIT WIDGEON GRASS

March 30, 1993

At a recent City Council meeting the question was asked, "What ever happened to the aquatic plant harvesting machine?"

The harvester (affectionately referred to as the "green machine" because of its color) was used extensively in the early '80s to cut and remove widgeon grass (genus *Ruppia*) from vast areas of the salt water lake.

The answer provides information on both recent Lake history and another reason to implement recommendation No.3 of the Lake Merritt Resource Enhancement Plan – "Replace Herbicide Use With Algal Pumping."

For two reasons, the harvester has been used much less frequently in recent years.

First, in 1985 most of the Lake was dredged (made deeper) to prevent the growth of widgeon grass which was covering more than half the surface of our urban estuary in June and July each year. The areal extent and surface of widgeon grass exposure were documented and mapped in the January, 1982, Final Report-Lake Merritt Restoration Project. Dredging to increase the water depth prevents widgeon grass from growing because light cannot penetrate to the bottom. This dredging was highly effective, and little widgeon grass has been seen in recent years.

The second reason that the harvester is not used much anymore is that beginning in 1987 an herbicide (aquazine - which has recently been removed from the market) has been applied every summer to control nuisance algal growth. It is probable that this chemical has reduced the growth of widgeon grass as well as control the blooms of algae that formerly choked the shallow shoreline area.

However, in July of 1991, I found two submerged areas of widgeon grass during a sonar survey for the Lake Merritt Siltation Study.

At this point we must dispel a common misconception.

The harvester is little used, indeed is not very effective, to control nuisance algae.

Enteromorpha, as the algae is known to scientists, is much too slippery and formless to be easily picked by the harvester. It simply slips off the cutting blades and conveyor belt. Also, the harvester cannot operate well in the shallow water (1 to 3 feet deep) where the algae grows. So, the harvester remains "on call" for potential widgeon grass problems, but cannot effectively control the algal blooms.

In April or May of this year, an herbicide treatment will occur to control the algae using stockpiled supplies from last year.

But this method of control is also likely to inhibit the growth of widgeon grass, which has been described as "one of the most valuable species of submerged aquatics in the whole country" (American Wildlife and Plants --- A guide to Wildlife Food Habits). Practically all parts of the plant are edible and consumed by waterfowl. For birds such as the coot, baldpate, gadwall, redhead, scaup and Canada goose, it can provide a tenth to a quarter of all their food needs. Herbicide could preclude the growth of this valuable plant everywhere in the lake (including the waterfowl refuge).

In 1993, after an initial herbicide application, algal pumping, as recommended in the Enhancement Plan, will be used on an experimental basis.

Algae from the shallow shoreline will be pumped (and broken up) as it is moved to deeper water where it will sink below the zone of light penetration, and be carried out by the tides. This method allows selective areas to be treated and it will not impact widgeon grass.

Algal pumping, even if done every day at high tide during the peak algal season, should cost less than the expensive chemical treatment, according to the Enhancement Plan.

A new era in algal treatment is beginning at Lake Merritt. Waterfowl, widgeon grass and Oakland will benefit.

Note: Algal pumping was replaced by harvesting using the city harvester, which (operated at high water level, and using a conveyor to pick up the algae), was found to be effective. But after it tipped over and was damaged, the city began contracting out the operation, which continues.

27. ANNUAL REPORT ON STATUS OF LAKE MERRITT RELEASED

May 18, 1993

The 1992 Lake Merritt Management Program Report has been published and awaits your review. Since 1988, these reports of water quality, algal control and related issues have been prepared by Engineering Science, Inc. under and ongoing contract with the Alameda County Department of Public Works – Division of Water Resources.

This program is funded by your tax money – through a special assessment for the Flood Control District. These documents summarize research and monitoring results, and provide an on-going basis to judge the health of our urban estuary.

Highlights of the 1992 report are presented below:

Nuisance algal growth in mid-to-late summer was well below normal after the herbicide treatment on May 15. Because surface mats of algae were not a problem in July, August, or September, the usual third, fourth and fifth herbicide treatments were not necessary.

The primary reasons for this period of slow growth are not fully understood, but appear to be related to overall reduction of algal growth in the San Francisco region during that time, and to the experimental "algal pumping" that occurred on June 1, 2 and 3 as part of the Lake Merritt Resource Enhancement Study.

The success of the pumping method led to recommendations in the 1992 report to conduct a combination of pumping and herbicide treatments in 1993.

As in previous years, dissolved oxygen levels in the estuary were adequate except near the two petrobarriers at the ends of Lake arms. There, oxygen concentrations at the bottom were typically 1.5 to 4.0 milligrams per liter (parts per million = ppm), which is below what is needed to sustain a healthy aquatic environment. At times, oxygen levels in these areas approached zero indicating anaerobic conditions which leads to foul odors and to the death of animals unable to move away from the area.

Even at the surface, oxygen levels were sometimes as low as 2.0 ppm near the two major storm drains areas.

Bacterial monitoring detected high levels of "indicator organisms" at the petrobarrier areas near the major storm drain outlets. These organisms indicate the potential presence of pathogenic bacteria (those that can cause human illness). Because pathogenic bacteria are very difficult to measure in water, indicator organisms are measured in their place. Because pathogens generally exist at levels about a thousand times lower than the indicator organisms, there is a built-in measure of safety by measuring the indicators.

The results show that you shouldn't swim near the ends of the Lake during many times of the year, but that the Lake center, beach area near Children's Fairyland, inlet/outlet area and 18th Street area, etc. are safe for water contact – except just after large rainfall events which wash lots of trash and bacteria in from the storm drains. During the summer, for most of the Lake, jump right in; it won't hurt you.

The annual fishery survey was conducted in October, and captured 121 fish comprising eight species. Most numerous were topsmelt (not related to the rare Delta smelt), followed in numbers by striped bass and shiner surfperch.

For the first time ever, a flatfish, the diamond turbot, was discovered. It was put on display at the Rotary Science aquarium, then released. Who knows, perhaps it's still out there.

To determine if herbicide or heavy metals are accumulating in Lake Merritt fish, samples of a striped bass and topsmelt were analyzed. No herbicide was found and only trace levels of mercury and zinc were detected in the fish. As in prior years, the concentrations were very low and do not indicate the presence of a health hazard to those who might eat these animals.

For copies of the 1992 Annual Report, contact the Alameda County Flood Control and Water Conservation District.

Note: County annual reports ceased in 1997.

28. LAKE ACTIVISTS UNITE: BEGIN VARIETY OF PROJECTS

June 1, 1993

Have you heard? Lake Merritt has a new, non-profit, educational, public interest, citizen/activist group dedicated to its preservation and enhancement. Finally, after 100 years, Oakland's natural resource "centerpiece" has an advocacy sponsor, dedicated to nourishing the natural values of the estuary and exploring their inter-relationship with people.

Created last summer, the Lake Merritt Institute (LMI) has met monthly over dinner at Zaa's restaurant, grown to several dozen members, sponsored a watershed clean-up, and been recognized by the City Council. Noted on the distinctive stationary are founding director William Penn Mott, Jr. (1909 – 1992), seven honorary directors and eight members of the board of directors.

Funds are being raised, and your support is encouraged. It has been said that if you want advice, ask for money; and if you want money, ask for advice. Therefore, we ask you: How should we implement enhancements at Lake Merritt?

One of the projects under consideration is an aeration fountain in memory of William Penn Mott, former director of the Oakland Office of Parks and Recreation, East Bay Regional Park District, and the National Park service. Such a fountain would not only beautify the Lake, it would add necessary oxygen to those areas where water quality standards are being violated by low oxygen conditions (Water Quality Control Board, are you listening?).

Projects underway or completed by LMI include: A Clean Up Campaign for the 4,000 acre watershed; public slide shows by Judge William McKinstry ("Historic Lake Merritt"), Dr. Richard Bailey ("The Lake Merritt Resource Enhancement Plan"), and Mr. Brooks Kolb ("The Proposed Lake Merritt Master Plan"); the Adopt a Storm Drain Program in the public schools; and support for the City's "We Mean Clean" and "Storm Drain Stenciling" programs.

LMI meetings are held every second Wednesday of the month at 552 Grand Avenue at 6 p.m. Anyone interested in education, research and improvement of Lake Merritt is cordially invited to attend. For further information, contact Kerry Jo Ricketts at the Oakland Office of Parks and Recreation at 238-2219.

The Lake Merritt Institute is open to anyone concerned about the future of this urban estuary. Will it be allowed to silt in and become a mud flat? Will public fishing (*a trout stocking program has been proposed) or wading (yes, it is safe in the summer) ever be allowed? Will the Master Plan ever be funded and implemented? If you join LMI, the answers may depend on you!

Note: The Lake Merritt Institute was founded in 1992 and continues working today (see back cover).

29. AN IMPORTANT MESSAGE OUT ON THE STREETS

June 18, 1993

They appeared last month in patriotic red, white, and blue on the sidewalks. Imperative statements: Educational messages repeated at seemingly random locations along Lake Shore, Grand and other avenues. No, its not graffiti, because on second glance, each sign is located above a storm drain. A storm drain that flows not to a treatment plant, not the to the Bay, not to a sanitary sewer, but directly to Lake Merritt. The meaning of the new painting on the sidewalks and curbs are clear: Anything that enters this opening in the street will end up in Lake Merritt.

Congratulations: You now know what only 13 percent of the population knew in a recent survey conducted by the Alameda County Department of Public Works. The other 87 percent thought that water (and trash etc.) entering the drains on every street went to some treatment plant where pollutants were removed. No. And not going to a treatment plant makes a big difference. That paper the other guy dropped on the sidewalk, the several thousand cigarette butts discarded daily, motor oil, used antifreeze etc. All have a direct, non-stop pipe to carry them right to the Lake. There, viewed by joggers, boaters, fish, and waterfowl, it all festers, robs the water of oxygen, and gradually fills in the Lake. Not only that, it looks bad, and it stinks.

The storm drain stencils were painted by a variety of volunteer groups using paint donated by a local business. Directing the program is the City of Oakland, Department of Public Works, in conjunction with the Alameda County Water Resources group. Storm drain stenciling is part of the Alameda County Urban Runoff Clean Water Program, a planning and implementation effort required nationwide by the federal Clean Water Act. Other communities in the Bay Area, Colorado and elsewhere are also labeling their storm drains in an effort to curb one of our most widespread and noxious sources of water pollution.

The stencils are in place, and more will be added through such efforts at the "Adapt a Storm Drain" program sponsored by the Lake Merritt Institute. The rest is up to citizens like you and me. Will the Saturday handyman get the message and stop dumping his used motor oil down the storm drain? Will the shop that empties it filthy mop bucket water put it in the sanitary sewer where it belongs? Will landowners take "Pride in Their Property" and spend 2-3 minutes a day cleaning up their section of pavement and gutter? We can hope, tell our neighbors, and do our part. Now that you know where the storm drain goes, please help keep Lake Merritt clean. For a free brochure, more details on urban runoff and Oakland's participation in the County program, call Surlene Grant at 238-3961, or Annie Fong at 238-6532.

Note: The City of Oakland is continuing the Adopt a Storm Drain program.

30. OAKLAND'S TIDAL ESTUARY MAY NEED LARGER PUMPS

July, 13, 1993

By now you know that Lake Merritt is not really a lake, but a tidal estuary. As such, it is connected to salt water, in this case the Oakland Estuary, San Francisco Bay, and the Pacific Ocean. That's right, anything that swims in the Pacific can swim right into downtown Oakland via Lake Merritt. Such is the source of our striped bass, leopard sharks, mermaids (?) and other migratory aquatic creatures.

But how do the tides get in and out? At the southeast corner of the Lake, under the 12th Street bridge, are tunnel culverts, constructed in 1927. Through them flow the cleansing tides, pulled by the moon which exerts a changing force as it moves around the earth and as the earth spins.

A full moon: Higher tides. A half-moon: Lower tides. Twice a day the Lake experiences a high tide, and twice a day the water ebbs low. Massive amounts of water (150 to 200 acre feet) flow through the tunnel between the higher high and lower low tide, replacing (on average) the entire volume of the Lake every four days.

The tunnels lead to the Lake Merritt channel, bordered in part by a parkland, and ending up at the Oakland Estuary. Along the way it passes under 10th Street, where it is restricted by eight narrow pipes, and is controlled by the 7th Street flood control pumps. Built in the late '60's in response to downtown flooding, these pumps can close off Lake Merritt from tidal flow, pump water in, or out. They allow high tides to be kept out when the Lake is filling with water from all those storm drains, provide a way to pump water out if we get too much rain, and protect us from flooding.

However, due to the constrictions, some flooding (from 4 to 6 feet) will occur during the 100 year flood, which will statistically occur once in 100 years. The pumping station also allows the Lake to be filled and kept full on weekends for regattas, festivals, algal control, etc. But wait a minute. Tides in the Bay sometimes vary 6 feet or more. Lake Merritt only rises and falls about 1 to 2 feet. Why? Restrictions and limited channel capacity limit the volume of water that can flow in or out during a tidal cycle. It's like trying to fill a bathtub with a straw in six hours; you can't do it.

These limits will also prevent rainfall from a flood larger than the 100 year flood from escaping the Lake. When this happens, low areas around the Lake will flood again. Even with the pumps, the channel is too small and too restricted to get rid of that much water that fast. Those narrow pipes under 10th Stret are the main impediment.

Enlarge them and (according to a tidal study in the recently completed Resource Enhancement Plan) more water will flow in and out, improving flood control. More water would also flush the Lake more, but his could also result in more exposed mud flats at low tides, and perhaps higher water at high tides.

The inlet-outlet channel: Oakland's direct connection to the Pacific Rim, a component of our flood control system, and the source of tides in Lake Merritt.

Note: The bottleneck pipes were removed as part of the 198 million dollar measure DD bond projects.

31. A KAYAK ADVENTURE ON LAKE MERRITT

August 10, 1993

"Hey, toss me that ball," said the voice from above on the 12th Street Bridge. There it was, floating on the water; a multi-colored ball just at the edge of the barrier that prevents objects from entering the inlet-outlet channel of Lake Merritt. I maneuvered the kayak to the edge of the barrier, retrieved the ball and flipped it to a guy on the bridge. But my aim was bad, and the ball fell back to the water beyond the barrier. It started moving with the current into the long, black tunnel.

"Wait, I'll get it," I said, wanting to redeem myself for the bad throw. Ignoring the current flowing into the tunnel, I pulled the kayak over the barrier and reached for the ball, now just out of reach. Missed. But being a college-educated primate, I used a tool by extending the paddle to pull in the recalcitrant prize. But it was still too far away, so I grasped the very tip of the paddle, leaned far out and (you guessed it) dropped the paddle. I didn't have a spare.

By this time the ball had entered the tunnel, moving steadily under the bridge toward the Oakland Estuary, a mile distant. Following it beyond reach was the paddle, my only means of locomotion. I knew from experience that on the other side of the channel the water flowed through small pipes, far too small to pass a boat, and maybe too small to pass a person. Any object too large to pass would be trapped against the pipes under the bridge while the water slowly rose with the tide until the air space was gone. It would not be a pretty place to spend the rest of one's life.

So, decision time: Leave the paddle go, or enter the tunnel to retrieve it. I really wanted that paddle, but fear was keeping me out of that black hole, and it was drifting further away. If I went in, could I get back out?

This was the maiden voyage for the new kayak, and my first time in such a vessel. With me was my 5 year old son, who was getting apprehensive about being so near to such a yawning cavern which appeared to have no end at the other side. Kids have a second sense about such places, and they instinctively avoid them.

The channel itself carries the tides both in and out of the Lake, its water level rising and falling 1 to 3 feet in height twice a day. At a 6 foot tide, the water gushes out so fast that you couldn't paddle against it. Hidden beneath the surface of the Lake, this tidal current has cut a canyon that hardly anybody knows about. Mapped as part of the Lake Merritt Silt Study, it measures 3 to 9 feet deeper than the adjacent bottom, is 40 to 100 feet wide, and extends 150 feet out into the Lake. The bottom here is scoured shell, not the soft mud that covers the other areas where currents are mild.

The new wooden paddle had been made in Oregon, and had cost me more than $90 just the week before. Seizing the moment, I let the current carry us in, and pushed against the walls of the tunnel to overtake the distant object. "NO!" screamed the 5 year old as the daylight faded away. I calmed him and wondered what the kid on the bridge thought when he saw the boat disappear under the street. Worse yet, I wondered what would happen if they started the pumps while I was in there. Naw, those guys don't work on Sundays; do they? A little further and … there, I had it. It was too narrow to turn the boat so, using the walls of the tunnel, I pushed us out back into the Lake and daylight. It had been easy, sort of safe, really – but I would rather not do it again, thank you. Mobile again, we quickly paddled away along the shoreline among the ducks.

For those whose interests about the inlet / outlet tunnel have been piqued by this episode, a future article will cover how the channel limits tidal flows, restricts flood control, and what is on the other side of the bridge.

Note: The small, multiple tunnels at 12th Street have since been replaced by one large tunnel that extends to the entire width of the channel to improve tidal circulation.

32. WHAT IF THE LAKE WAS STOCKED WITH RAINBOW TROUT?

August 20, 1993

The line went taut and the rod bowed. But when the young fisherman tried to reel him in, the big fish wouldn't budge. (This was no ordinary trout). After battle that lasted 10 minutes, a trophy size rainbow was pulled into the boat, and taken to the dock to be weighed. It was, the newspaper said, a new record. Unfortunately, it was caught at Lake Merced in San Francisco, not at Lake Merritt in Oakland. Lake Merced is stocked with trout, and supports a valuable urban fishery. Lake Merritt is not stocked, and few people try their luck.

What if Lake Merritt were stocked with rainbow trout? What if Oakland's youth had the opportunity to catch a fish downtown, and bring it home for supper? Ah, the fish wouldn't live in salt water, a disbeliever said. But rainbow trout are the same as steelhead, which is a migratory form that moves between salt and fresh water. To test the theory, a state Department of Fish and Game truck delivered several dozen hatchery trout to Lake Merritt several years ago, where they were held in a pen next to the sailboat house dock. After two days, the fish were fine. Most were released, and two were later seen in the Lake Merritt channel heading for the Bay.

But Lake Merritt is polluted and the fish wouldn't be good to eat, said another pessimist. Lake Merritt is not polluted. Although bacterial counts are high after rainfall events, tidal action quickly flushes the Lake and returns bacterial counts to levels below that of concern. The last three years of bacterial monitoring have shown that in the summer, water quality is adequate for body contact sports such as swimming and wind surfing.

Even after a rain, the bacteria in water do not make fish unsafe for eating because the microorganisms are not incorporated into fish flesh. Proper cleaning and cooking provide further safeguards, and these issues could be verified by the county Health Department. What about metal contamination from the storm drain sediments? Some of those sediments are high in lead, but native fish in Lake Merritt have been tested for metals, and the levels are not of concern.

Stocked fish, raised in a hatchery, would have even lower levels, and would not pick up contamination in the short time they would be in the Lake before being caught, eaten by cormorants, or migrating out to the sea. Two real limitations are temperature (it may be too warm in the summer) and cormorants (which are very numerous in the fall). Cormorants are known to eat 6 to 8 inch trout, and might wipe out a hatchery load in a few days. A pilot project would provide more data on these issues.

Actually, the real barriers to stocking lake Merritt are political. Fears about overcrowding the Lake, snagging pedestrians, hooking seagulls, and funding the program were quickly raised when I proposed the idea several years ago. Each of these concerns, can be overcome. By restricting fishing to those with a city permit, overcrowding can be prevented. Permits could be given mainly to youth, and the elderly or the disadvantaged, and could be given only after an hour of training by staff from the Rotary Science Center, or from the Science and Art Integrated at the Lake (SAIL) staff. This training would instill a respect for the Lake, teach how to avoid hooking people and birds, and instruct participants on the rules of the program.

By restoring the dilapidated docks with safety rails, educational signs and benches, safe fishing piers could be established, and would be used by non-fishermen as well. To me, the benefits of such a program far outweigh its minor cost of planning and implementation. A youth who catches a fish in Lake Merrit will develop a respect not only for our downtown estuary, but also for natural resources in general.

Such is the attraction of catching a fish that, given the opportunity to go fishing or hang out or do drugs, many of Oakland's young people will choose to go fishing. The State Department of Fish and Game was willing to try stocking the fish: Is Oakland ready to support such a program?

Note: A Fishing in the City Program was begun at the lake and rainbow trout were stocked several times. Although popular, the program was not continued.

33. WILDLIFE THREATENED AS MERRITT SHORE ERODES

August 27, 1993

Situated between the two arms of Lake Merritt in downtown Oakland is a peninsula. Within this peninsula are Lakeside Park, Children's Fairyland, the Rowboat House, Garden Center, and other popular attractions. This special place (surrounded on two sides by water) provides an unusual vista of reflected high rises, and the relaxing atmosphere of a large scenic park.

Like Central Park in New York or Lincoln Park in Chicago, this place is unique. Where else can you find a 160 tidal estuary surrounded by downtown? Where else do geese hatch within sight of high rises, or flocks of wild ducks and schools of fish thrive in such an urban setting?

In general, this unique area is landscaped, watered and without many of the ills that plague other parts of the metropolis. But on the western side, a serious problem is evident. The area is slowly shrinking. Buffeted by waves from the long fetch of open water, and scoured by waterfalls from above, it is steadily eroding into the Lake. The evidence (uprooted trees, collapsed bulkheads and barren soil) is unmistakable. As the near vertical face of the cliff retreats, small patches of land protected by bulkheads protrude several feet out into the Lake. But at the unprotected areas (along 700 feet of shoreline) waves at high tide are slowly washing away the soil. This severely eroded area was studied under task five of the Lake Merritt Resource Enhancement Plan. A conclusion of the plan is that this area is one of the only natural shorelines along the Lake.

At most other shorelines, including the wildlife refuge islands, an artificial bulkhead prevails, limiting the natural slope where land meets water. Furthermore, it is the only natural shoreline in Lake Merritt not immediately adjacent to a foot path. As such, it is favored by wildlife. Egrets hunt without fear. Small fish escape the predators of deeper water, and the warmer shallows provide a natural nursery for shrimp, crabs, and worms.

Because this is the only natural shoreline not adjacent to a footpath, a new bulkhead should not be the favored solution to erosion at this location. How then should we stop the problem of trees falling into the Lake, and the eventual loss of land perhaps as far back as the path, now many feet distant? The Enhancement Plan recommends two solutions.

First, a high salt marsh should be built along the shallow shoreline shelf to quell wave action. The small marsh, about 15 -20 feet wide, would be protected on the outside by a low berm, and separated from the shore by a channel. It would provide the key wetland habitat now missing in the Lake, as well as solve the wave erosion problem.

The second solution recommended is an erosion control project above and on the cliff. Here, a fence should prevent pedestrians from trampling the vegetation and slipping down the steep slopes. Shallow terraces of new soil should be built over the eroded roots, and planted with native species. Runoff would be directed away from the cliff by a diversion channel, and erosion proof material would be used to stabilize the steeper areas.

Taken together, these measures would eliminate the erosion, and significantly improve wildlife habitat. The erosion problem is real, and becomes more severe each year. A solution exists, but a commitment from concerned citizens and government, and funding, is needed.

Note: This project was not completed, but small, high salt marsh wetlands have been created at the boating center parking lot, and along the channel. The latter have been frequently vandalized.

34. WHY NOT A "LAKEKEEPER"?

September 28, 1993

San Francisco Bay has a Baykeeper: Why not Lake Merritt? Dedicated to preserving the health of Lake Merritt's parent estuary," the Baykeeper patrols San Francisco Bay, educates about pollution, and lobbies for Bay protection. Not surprisingly, these functions are also needed for Lake Merritt. What would a Lakekeeper do? The following list barely scratches the surface.

Keep the Lake Clean. As a full-time employee, the Lakekeeper would insure that trash is removed as soon as possible, including on weekends and during stormwater runoff events. As an individual personally re-sponsible for keeping the Lake clean, the Lakekeeper would eventually begin to recognize the sources of pollution, and provide feedback to en-forcement agencies. As individuals we would all benefit from this action. So would real estate values.

Educate Citizens and Government. Major Lake issues face the City Coun-cil and citizen's groups. Should they accept algal pumping or try to get a new herbicide approved? Should fishing and wading continue to be pro-hibited or allowed under certain circumstances? Where is the line be-tween enjoyment of a natural resource, and overuse? The Lakekeeper would be knowledgeable of existing information (most people don't know what is known) and be able to generate new data upon request. As the ombudsman for the Lake, he or she would testify at hearings, make presentations to groups, and prepare press releases.

Raise Funds. There are a lot of grants out there, more than can be ap-plied for by even such dedicated staff as Kerry Jo Ricketts of Oakland Parks and Recreation. In addition to a needy cause such as Lake Merritt, it takes full time involvement, commitment, and detailed knowledge to win a grant. By spending one day a week and working in conjunction with such groups as the Lake Merritt Institute, the Lakekeeper would eventually bring in funds to repair docks, dredge polluted sediments, im-prove water quality monitoring, and perhaps even establish a flow through aquarium for educational purposes.

Patrol the Waters and Shoreline. Safety and security could be enhanced by a Lakekeeper on patrol in a boat and on shore. Using a cellular phone and video cameras as a deterrent, purveyors of crime could be convinced to go elsewhere. Just knowing that they may be watched by a distant camera aboard a boat would be enough to deter breaking into a car or doing a drug deal. By focusing patrols at certain times and locations, elderly residents would feel safer walking in the park, and vandalism could be reduced.

Monitor the Waters and Life Forms.

What's really out there? In the last three years leopard sharks and the first flatfish were discovered in Lake Merritt. Tubeworms have disappeared, but why? Are waterfowl numbers stable, or at risk from disease such as caused the recent controversial removal of ducks in the Los Angeles area? What breeds in the Lake, and do salmon and herring still come in attempting to spawn? Some even say there is more than one mermaid out there.

Corporate Sponsorship is needed. It's all possible; all that is needed is funding for the position. The Lakekeeper could be established as an employee of a non-profit group such as the Lake Merritt Institute, and be responsible to the Board of Directors, the city, and the director of the funding source. Funding would likely be tax-deductible, and the publicity benefits would be enormous. Recent and projected funding cuts make it clear that government alone cannot provide the extent of support required to keep Lake Merritt from deteriorating. If the greatest natural resource in the city is to be maintained and improved, we need a Lakekeeper.

Note: The Waterkeeper Alliance, founded by Robert F. Kennedy Jr., demanded that the Lake Merritt Institute cease using the term Lakekeeper because LMI was not a group that filed legal actions. LMI reluctantly complied.

35. PINPOINTING SOURCE OF GLEN ECHO CREEK POLLUTION

October 19, 1993

It happened again on Aug. 2: A creamy discoloration covering the entire surface of Glen Echo Creek up to the containment boom at Lake Merritt. Although this pollution has likely been going on for years, authorities are beginning to close in on the sources. Thanks to the letters and photographs from a concerned citizen, there now exists documented proof of the water quality violations.

In late October of 1992, late April of 1993, and on August 2, 1993, thick, black oil, a light surface oily sheen or milky emulsion have been recorded on the waters of Glen Echo Creek where it emerges from the storm drain near the corner of Grand and Harrison. Speculation on the sources has included disinfectants such as Lysol or pine oil which emulsify in water, creating a milky white mixture. Likely culprits for the black oil and floating sheen are auto repair garages and/or thoughtless street mechanics who pour their poisonous chemicals down storm drains.

Whoever they are, the probably don't know that their storm drains empty into Lake Merritt. But ignorance of the law is no excuse, and when enforcement personnel come knocking at the door, fines will be levied. The California Regional Water Quality Control Board has been notified, as have Oakland city officials.

Since the Water Board has only a handful of inspectors for the entire Bay Area, don't expect to see a team of scientists out there taking water samples any time soon. But the Board is asking questions: After all, this is Lake Merrit, not just any storm drain case. The squeaky wheel gets the grease, and this one is squeaking in their own back yard. State officials at the Regional Board are talking to Public Works inspectors, and to law enforcement personnel. People care about Lake Merritt, and this resource is one that will not be easily yielded to the dastardly dumpers.

Glen Echo pollution is of interest to City Council and the Lake Merritt Institute as well as the concerned citizen that has recorded pollution events. They are tired of seeing the oily smudges coming out of the creek and the big storm drain along Harrison Avenue. Like bulldogs after a bone, they don't intend to let go.

For other reasons, this is no small matter. During the Lake Merritt Resource Enhancement Study, total petroleum hydrocarbons in the motor oil range were measured at 1,880 parts per million (dry weight basis) in Lake Merritt sediments combined from the storm drain areas at the mouth of Glen Echo Creek and Trestle Glen area. This high level indicates an oil pollution problem, and (if you are a clam or crab trying to live there) it is obnoxious. Even worse, lead levels in the sediments from Glen Echo alone were measured at 1,100 ppm, above the 1,000 ppm hazardous limit.

If confirmed by additional studies, these levels would make disposal of these sediments (which badly need to be dredged out) a very expensive proposition. Why should Oakland taxpayers have to pay for disposal of hazardous sediments because of illegal dumpers? They shouldn't; and the city is now investigating potential sources by testing storm drains and conducting surprise inspections. Violators have been caught, and more will be added to the list.

So, if it's your pollution that fouls Glen Echo Creek and Lake Merritt, clean up your act; or wait for the knock at the door. If you own or work in a business in the Lake Merritt watershed (especially north and northeast Oakland, and Piedmont), are you certain all material put in drains does not go to Lake Merritt? If you are not sure, and want to find out, call Oakland Public Works at 238-3051. They can help you avoid the knock at the door.

Note: Pollution from Glen Echo creek continues to enter Lake Merritt.

36. ONLY PUBLIC INVOLVEMENT WILL MAKE LAKE IMPROVEMENTS A REALITY

November 23, 1993

In 1992 the Lake Merritt Resource Enhancement Plan was completed. The plan recommended 20 projects and additions to enhance Lake Merritt, focusing on water quality improvement, wildlife habitat enhancement, and strengthening the relationship between the city and its unique downtown estuary. In early 1993 the City Council accepted the Enhancement Plan, which had been prepared under the guidance of the Office of Parks and Recreation. The following is a summary of actions that have been taken (or not taken) to implement the plan.

Only the six highest-priority recommendations are discussed in detail. To obtain a copy of the remaining recommendations, contact the Office of Parks and Recreation.

The number one priority was implemented when the Lake Merritt Institute (a non-profit, public interest group dedicated to the improvement of the Lake and its environs) was formed. Meetings are held every third Wednesday at the Lake Merrit Hotel at 5:30 p.m. (call Chairperson Win Walsh at 568-6959 for meeting information). Without this advocacy group, the enhancement Plan would likely remain a document on the Shelf, a victim of budget cuts, bureaucratic indifference, and ignorance of what could be accomplished.

Dredging of the storm drain sediments (priority #5) and installation of an aeration fountain (#2) were discussed in recent Montclarion articles. Dredging awaits a city / county agreement on funding. It is essential if we are to maintain Lake Merritt as on open body of water. The fountain is a current topic of discussion while fund-raising efforts are proceeding. It is proposed that the fountain be dedicated to the memory of William Penn Mott, Jr., a former director of Oakland Parks and Recreation, and of the United States Department of the Interior.

"Replace Herbicide Use with Algal Pumping" was the third-highest priority. During the summer of 1993 algal pumping was used in conjunction with herbicide to control nuisance levels of shoreline algae, and the combination will used again in 1994. After that, the stockpiled supply of aquazine herbicide will be used up, and since this chemical is no longer manufactured for use in aquatic environments, it will not be available. Although as effective, algal pumping is more labor intensive, and the overall dollar costs are about the same as chemical use.

In my opinion, environmental (total) costs of algal pumping are significantly lower than those of chemical use. Algal pumping does not affect the wildlife refuge, widgeon grass, or phytoplankton, which are all key features of the food chain.

"Create High Salt Marsh Wetland Habitats" was the number four priority. This recommendation proposed that four small (total 2.3 acres) of marsh areas be established. The wetlands would be high salt marshes, dominated by the plants pickleweed, salt grass and gum plant. In two areas they would stabilize existing areas of significant erosion.   Material dredged from the Lake would be too contaminated to be used for these marshes, but clean material would not be expensive. All four areas would be along the shoreline and away from boat traffic. They would re-establish habitats formerly abundant in the Lake, enhance visual diversity, and provide homes for species not now able to live in the nation's first wildlife refuge.

"Incorporate Enhancement Plan Results into the Master Plan Process" was the number six priority. The proposed master plan for the Lake and its surrounding area is the subject of meetings by a committee appointed to develop the concept, which grew out of the Community Assistance Team study completed in 1989. Actual creation of this plan has been stymied by a lack of funding, which has led to consideration of doing individual components of the plan separately. Committee members are aware of the Enhancement Plan recommendations, which are proceeding while the Master Plan is being further developed.

Conclusion: Eight of the 20 recommendations have been implemented or are in the process of implementation. In the top six category, only marsh creation has received no further work. The remaining 12 await commitment, personnel, and funding, but may fall victim to the "Raiders of the Last Park" (ignorance, greed, apathy, and self-interest). Only with a continued and increased level of effort by citizens in concert with city officials and politicians (and a commitment on their part) will the complete Resource Enhancement Plan be realized.

Each of us can help. To support a particular project, write or call the mayor and your council member; contact the Office of Parks and Recreation or Public Works, and send a letter to the editor. To really get involved, contact the Lake Merritt Institute at 1520 Lakeside Drive, 94612 (238-2219). Your help can make a visible difference, one that will bring lasting satisfaction and recognition.

Note: Regarding the top six recommendations: The Lake Merritt Institute was created; fountains were installed; algal pumping was accomplished by harvesting; marsh restoration was partly accomplished; limited area dredging was done in 1997; and the Master Plan, which focused on more widespread, land based planning, adapted some of the Enhancement Plan recommendations.

37. LAKE MERRITT'S SEDIMENT PROBLEM GROWS

November 9, 1993

The storm drain areas of Lake Merritt need to be dredged. In fact, they desperately need to be dredged. Every winter mounds of street runoff, chemicals, leaves, and garbage accumulate at the ends of the storm drains. And every summer this accumulated debris spreads out over the entire lake bottom, carrying its load of contaminants with it. Oil and grease, lead and oxygen consuming organic matter combine to suffocate and poison the bottom.

At times in the spring the sediment at El Embarcadero depletes so much of the water's oxygen that it can't be measured. Wildlife suffers. And then there is the putrid hydrogen sulfide (rotten eggs) odor that joggers of the lakeshore path know only too well. It comes from the sediment that is slowly filling up Lake Merritt, creating a mud flat laden with oil and heavy metals. If Oakland wants to keep Lake Merritt, sediment needs to be dredged.

Annually since 1989 the recommendations to dredge have been made. In the Water Quality Monitoring reports, in the Sediment Study, and in the Enhancement Plan, the rationale and details have been presented. Diagrams of the areas where sediment should be removed, chemical analysis of the material, and two cost estimates were presented to the city in September of 1992. City and county public works officials know full well that these areas have needed to be dredged for several years. In fact, the sediment should be removed at least every two years to prevent it from migrating out over the entire bottom. The Lake Merritt storm drain areas should have been dredged in 1989, 1991 and 1993. What is happening?

Alameda County and the City of Oakland are trying to reach an agreement as to who is most responsible (i.e. who pays how much). Because the city owns the Lake and the county is responsible for the storm drain runoff, an agreement is needed before dredging can occur. Such an agreement is possible (these two agencies worked together when the Lake was last dredged in 1985). But when money is tight, it is easier to disagree. Talks have been held, but no one has applied for the permits, and funding has not been finalized. The schedule is still loose, and the county has developed their own (higher) estimates of cost, which are being debated.

In this time of environmental concern, when the citizens (who elect the public officials) are demanding that pollution be cleaned up, and are willing to pay for it, the delays have gone on long enough. With each rainfall the contamination builds.

Are you a Lake Merritt activist (one who cares about the lake and is active)? Do you want the bureaucratic log jam broken and the storm drain sediments dredged? If so, call Don Labelle, Director of Public Works at Alameda County, 670-5455; and call Terry Roberts, Director of the Oakland Public Works Department, 238-3961. Tell them you want a city/county agreement by Christmas (this year) and dredging in the early autumn of 1994. Be prepared for the usual delays, but don't accept them. Oakland has a right to a healthy Lake Merritt, and if the bureaucrats can't agree, ask them to move over.

Better yet, call or write your County Commissioner and City Council person. Tell hem to call Labelle and Roberts, and demand that: (1) A timetable be established for the agreement and dredging; (2) The permit application process be started; (3) Sources of funding be found or set aside (grants, private donations, government funds, etc.); (4) Plans be made for dredging every two years so we don't have to go through all this again in 1995. Tell them you don't want Lake Merritt to turn into a mud flat of storm drain runoff. If enough people call, we'll get action. If not, watch the Lake, its shoreline real estate values, its recreational potential, and its wildlife all suffer.

Note: Despite having been dredged an average of every 11 years since 1893, Lake Merritt has not been dredged since 1997, twenty seven years ago.

38. THE CASE OF THE MISSING *MERCIERELLA*

December 7, 1993

They used to be common everywhere in the Lake; small white tubes housing even smaller worms. But today they are hard to find, almost non-existent. Biologists from nearby universities used to collect them from docks to study in their classrooms. But when I last spoke with one of these teachers, she said the worms had all but disappeared.

Scientists that use Latin names call them *Mercierella*, which is the scientific name given to only this genus. What those that spoke Latin called them is anybody's guess since these people no longer exist, but because it is the name of a genus (the next wider grouping above a species), the first letter is capitalized. Because it is a scientific name, the genus is italicized.

It all sounds more complicated than it should, until you realize that knowing the Latin genus of animals allows you to communicate with other scientists about exactly the same creature, no matter where it is found. There are lots of different fish called "rock fish" and lots of different birds called "warbler." But when you know the genus of a plant or animal, the doors to all of what science knows about it are opened. Names give us power, especially when they are scientific names.

The mystery is: Where have all the *Mercierella* gone? Their loss has not gone unnoticed by Dick Kaufmann and other rangers at the Rotary Nature Center on the Lake, and there are several theories. One is that the herbicide used to control summer algae is somehow responsible. The tubeworm disappearance seemed to coincide with the start of herbicide use in 1988. The herbicide was used fewer times last summer, and will be used sparingly again in 1994 as the supply will run out. Assuming that herbicide use is eliminated in 1995 and beyond, it will be interesting to see if the worms return.

Another theory is the long drought, which began in 1986-87. Less rain may have made the water more saline, perhaps changing the ability of the worms to breed or survive.

Still a third possibility is the invasion of an Asian clam (a non-native species), which could have usurped all the available habitat formerly occupied by *Mercierella.*

My guess is that the invading clams (which like most exotic species, arrived without their typical predators, parasites, and diseases to control their population) have displaced the tubeworms. One can see these clams in the shallows just below the high tide line where *Mercierella* used to be. It would not be the first time that an introduced species dislodged a native species.

But if competition with the clam is the reason for their disappearance from the Lake, they should still be found where the clam has not taken over, such as on the grates of the flood control pumps in the Lake Merritt Channel. Under water videos taken in November of 1993, however, do not show any clear shots of tubeworm growth.

If the drought and resultant increase in salinity were the cause, this would also explain tubeworm absence at the flood control gates. However, we have had two years of normal rain, and they have not repopulated. Native species are well adapted to recovery once normal conditions return, and they should be here by now.

As for the herbicide theory, it could be that something specific in the biochemistry of this tubeworm is incompatible with the simazine that kills algae. This interaction could be specific only to this tubeworm since we have determined that the herbicide does not accumulate in, and apparently does not harm the waterfowl, fish or mussels that have been tested. But if the herbicide has caused the decline, this is one more reason for the city to switch to algal pumping as a method of controlling the nuisance levels of these plants.

We don't know enough about the role of these tubeworms in the community to evaluate the effects of their loss on other animals in the Lake. Are they eaten by something else? If so, are they an important part of their diet? Did the worm's water filtration activities have any impact on water quality? These questions require dedicated research, something we seem to have less of each year.

However, their loss alerts us to the fact that something has changed. It is up to us to find out what has changed and (if appropriate and possible) to respond.

Note: This tubeworm still grows in Lake Merritt.

39. FORUM SET TO DISCUSS POSSIBLE LAKE MERRITT FOUNTAIN

November 2, 1993

Will there be a fountain at Lake Merritt? Previous Montclarion articles have discussed the need for such an aeration device (Sept. 27, 1991) and presented the results of an engineering study that proved it would work (May 19, 1992).

The Lake Merritt Institute is very interested in establishing fountains at the ends of the Glen Echo and Trestle Glen arms of the Lake in honor of William Penn Mott, Jr. The Lake Merritt Breakfast Club (Lake Committee) is also investigating a fountain, and has obtained cost estimates.

In the Lake Merritt Enhancement Plan which was approved by the City Council this year, installation of an aeration fountain was highly recommended to:

- Alleviate low oxygen problems
- Provide aesthetic enhancement
- Improve habitat for fish, waterfowl, and invertebrates

The hang-ups seem to be: "What is aesthetic enhancement?" and "We don't have the money." Concerns have been expressed by the city's Office of Parks and Recreation that such a device would be controversial, that the sound of falling water could be objectionable, and that pedestrians might get wet. They wonder if bubblers might not be a better idea.

The Office of Public Works is worried about the cost of electrical connections and maintenance costs. There is also one influential individual who is opposed to a fountain, apparently because he doesn't like the idea. A public meeting on Lake Merritt issues will be held Wednesday, Nov. 10 and the fountain will be a topic of discussion. At this forum, citizens are likely to hear proposals ranging from a minimal one-horsepower unit with a single spray, to a five horsepower 26-foot-high "rocket" surrounded by five sunburst fountains. Capital costs would range from $5,000 for each of two fountains in the smallest proposal to $34,560 for the multi-spray unit. Operating costs would range from $1,180 per year for electricity and annual oil changes for a one-horsepower unit to at least $12,000 for the rocket/sunburst combination.

Given the amounts now spent on landscape maintenance, these figures do not seem out of line for water quality improvement. As was the case with the necklace of lights, it is very likely that funds could be raised from private sources to minimize city expenditures.

The big questions are: 1) What do city officials want? And 2) How will we know what the citizens want? Short of doing a specific survey, the public meeting is the only planned formal method for obtaining public input to decision makers. But to some extent, a survey has already been done. In 1988, as part of the CAT (Community Assistance Team) study, people were given a questionnaire asking their views on Lake Merritt and the surrounding area.

When asked what the negative aspects of the lake environment were, the second-highest response was to the "stench" at the ends of the lake (which is where the fountains are proposed). The fountains could allevi- ate this concern.

By increasing the amount of oxygen in the water, fountains that spray surface or mid-depth water into the air would reduce this stench, which typically comes from anaerobic decomposition of organic matter in the sediment. The increased oxygen reduces hydrogen sulfide, the most ob- noxious of the gases produced.

Bubblers, on the other hand, typically disperse air from near the bottom, and while oxygenating the water, are more likely to re-suspend bottom sediment, which can be odorous. Spray fountains, therefore, would be more likely to eliminate odors than bubbler aerators.

If public opinion favors a fountain, how big should it be? Should there be one at the end of each arm where the low-oxygen problems exist? Should it have lights? How about colored lights or a changing pattern of colored lights? Do people want a bubbler, or how high should the water spray? These are questions that need answers.

Pilot Project Proposed: Why not install a pilot project fountain for one month and see if people like it? The Lake Merritt Institute may be able to assist with the costs of electrical hook-up, and people could view the real thing and provide comments. If you have a viewpoint on installing a fountain at Lake Merritt to improve low-oxygen conditions and provide an aesthetic enhancement, write to your local newspaper, and send a copy to the Lake Merritt Institute at 1520 Lakeside Drive, Oakland, 94612.

And, if you can, attend the public meeting on Nov. 10. Consider the value of Lake Merritt to Oakland, and decide if the water quality is worth improving.

Note: As many as four locations had fountains in recent years, but changing water levels and siltation rendered them inoperable.

40. FORUM DISCUSSES IMPROVING LAKE MERRITT

December 14, 1993

Aeration to improve low oxygen conditions and odors, creation of a small, demonstration high salt marsh, and establishment of natural shoreline areas emerged as preferences for improving Lake Merritt, participants at a public forum concluded last week. Sponsored by the Lake Merritt Master Plan Committee with assistance from the Oakland Environmental Affairs Commission, Parks and Recreation Advisory Commission and the Lake Merritt Institute, the meeting was called to solicit public opinion regarding proposed restoration, maintenance, and enhancement projects.

Identifying a single (or perhaps two) projects that would be non-controversial and able to be included in next year's city budget was a key objective of the gathering. Twelve potential projects were discussed and were eventually the subject of an opinion poll.

John Russo, chair of the city Environmental Affairs Commission, moderated the session, guiding participants around potentially divisive issues while allowing all points of view to be expressed. Anne Woodell, Stana Hearne and Diane Heinze gave introductions and briefly discussed the roles of the co-sponsoring groups. Speakers included Brooks Kolb, chairman of the Master Plan Committee, and Dr. Richard Bailey, author of the Lake Merritt Resource Enhancement Plan.

Using a system of first, second, and third choice votes, 19 of the attendees indicated rather clean preferences among the projects. Foremost in the ranking was aeration in areas where storm drain deposits deplete oxygen and cause odors. This option received 16 total votes, including 10 first place choices. Second in preference was a demonstration salt marsh, probably in an area between offshore islands at the wildlife refuge. This proposal earned 11 votes, including five first place selections.

Creation of a more natural shoreline area in some areas (perhaps where bulkheads are now failing) got seven votes, two of them being first choices.

The other projects on the list and the number of votes received were: Bandstand restoration (six); improvement of the perimeter path (five); tree plantings (four); dredging the storm drain sediment (two); installation of informational signs (two); installing educational signs (one); and repair of the bulkheads with similar concrete structures (zero).

Three of the projects (aeration, marsh, and dredging) have been evaluated by the Resource Enhancement Plan, and approved by the City Council in early 1993. Nine of the projects were recommendations in the Community Assistance Team Study which led to the formation of the Master Plan Committee.

Discussion of the aeration proposal centered on use of a fountain, or a bubbler. According to the memorandum by an engineering firm, both would supply adequate oxygen for the limited areas where the low oxygen is a severe problem. Due to city staff potential concerns over the functionality of an aeration device, more technical comments will be solicited. The issue will be discussed at the Jan. 19 meeting of the Lake Merritt Institute, to be held at the Lake Merrit Hotel at 5:30.

Concerns were expressed that project costs should be a determinant in deciding project preferences because several projects (e.g. aeration, signs, sand, and tree plantings) might be accomplished for the cost of one expensive project (the city projects bandstand restoration will cost about $320,000).

The issue is complicated because some projects could be more readily funded (the Lake Merritt Institute has a grant of $2,500 for a fountain), and political controversy is probably as much (if not more) of a deterrent.

Note: Several of these projects were completed as part of the Measure DD bond program. Aeration devices continue be studied as part of a two year pilot project. Limited area dredging was done in 1997, but is now overdue for those same areas.

41. A WINDOW OF LAKE MERRITT MAY BE SEEN

December 21, 1993

Some of the most exotic residents of Lake Merritt are never seen. Even though they occupy 160 acres of prime downtown real estate, they remain out of sight, hidden from daily view. There is a potential way to observe them, but recent plans have called for it's elimination. The elusive residents are leopard sharks, pipefish, sting rays, anemones and sponges which live beneath the waters of Lake Merritt. Here they go about their existence, unseen and unknown.

 The potential way to observe them could be the 90-gallon aquarium at the Rotary Science Center. Unfortunately, the aquarium is not part of the plans to remodel the science center. Deficient in necessary equipment and lacking the maintenance to be attractive, the aquarium sits largely ignored in the exhibit hall. The glass is hard to see through; it looks dirty; and there doesn't seem to be anything alive in it. Although it has a power pump, there is no light, no bubbles, and no visible fish. This "mirror of Lake Merritt" has been neglected for years, and is not a good visible representation of our estuary.

It doesn't have to be that way. For a few hundred dollars, basic aquarium equipment could be purchased and installed in minutes. An afternoon of cleaning and new crushed shell for the bottom would create an attractive and functional educational exhibit. Minimum equipment needed: A fluorescent light; power filter (proper size for the number of gallons); air pump, valves, and air stones; hydrometer (to measure specific gravity — which tells you the salinity); and a how-to-do-it book from the pet shop.

Once a week some of the water would have to be replaced with fresh lake water, and the glass would have to be scraped. Put the light on a timer, change the filter once in a while, add critters and presto; instant public interest, good public relations, and an opportunity to educate children about the world in which we live (much more interesting than doing drugs).

Perhaps student volunteers could be utilized. With all the budget cutbacks and retirements, the overworked rangers at the Science Center could certainly use the help. Perhaps the SAIL program (Science and Art Integrated at the Lake) could step in and rescue the doomed exhibit. There is talk of establishing a mini marine laboratory at the Boat House to monitor the living creatures in, on, and below the waters.

If the aquarium were functional, it could display some of these living forms. In the early spring, schools of half inch fish could be displayed; in late spring and early summer, widgeon grass could be collected; crabs and mussels and clams could be shown all year round. An occasional unusual fish could be exhibited, as was done with the first flatfish ever caught in the lake.

This basic system would however, have one weakness. The aquarium water would become too warm for many of the lake residents, which are acclimated the cool (seldom over 70 degrees F) tidal water from the San Francisco Bay and Pacific Ocean. Some of them would not survive long, and could only be displayed for a day or two. The solution: A flow through aquarium like the professional exhibits at Monterey and Golden Gate Park. If San Francisco can pump sea water all the way from the ocean to its aquarium, why can't Oakland pump it 200 feet to the Rotary Science Center? All that would be needed would be a submersible pump, plastic pipe, filter, and electricity. With this system, the aquarium would be not just a mirror to the lake, but a "window."

Any and all of the aquatic life that would fit in the tank could be displayed, and with proper care and feeding (let's hatch some brine shrimp!) most would survive. In addition, a flow through aquarium would bring lake water within easy reach to continually monitor salinity, temperature, oxygen, and other features that are continually changing with the tides and seasons. Our knowledge of the century old body of water would expand by leaps and bounds.

If you would like to volunteer some time, stop by the Rotary Science Center (see Stephanie or Dick) and the Sail Boat House (talk to Kerry or Joe). Contributions in the form of equipment, especially a small submersible pump, would be gratefully acknowledged. In addition to knowing that thousands of people will benefit from your actions, it's tax deductible.

Note: The aquarium was moved to the Lake Merritt Institute, but later dismantled.

42. LAKE MERRITT REPRESENTS 10,000 YEARS OF EVOLUTION AND HISTORY

January 1, 1994

Long before man walked its shores, there existed an estuary we now call Lake Merritt. Formed by the same tidal forces that control it today, it has pulsed through the ages, fed countless flocks of waterfowl, and nourished our ancestors. Events such as fires, floods, and major earthquakes are trivial to the lake for she has seen them countless times: She will see them countless times again.

Our best estimates indicate that Lake was probably formed in the late Pleistocene more, more than 10,000 years ago. Temperatures warmed as the last ice age ended and the seas once again rose to flood what later became known as San Antonio Creek. As prominent as the tides were to her formation, were the creeks that brought fresh water to mingle with the sea. Recently called Glen Echo, Wilder, and Indian Gulch Creeks, they were then unnamed streams, fed by the still variable rains and home to spawning salmon along the redwood shores.

Some say that a few of the salmon ancestors still make the pilgrimage, seeking the lost gravel beds, homing into a signal imbedded in their genes. When the descendants of those people that crossed the Bering Straits first saw the estuary on their way to Central and South America, there were grizzly bear tracks on the mud, and elk on the overlooking hills.

Out in the Bay, seals were a common sight, and perhaps sea otters and gray whales. The abundance of wildlife would be astounding by today's standards. Unharvested, unpolluted, and undeveloped, the vast resources of time lay fertile and available. Broad marshlands, shimmering mud flats and rafts of ducks greeted these first human visitors. Fish, shellfish, deer and other game supplied most of the food for early residents, some of whom hunted and gathered along the shore of what became Lake Merritt.

Such was the very early history of Lake Merritt. The records lie buried in geological strata and on the dusty shelves of libraries at nearby universities. That these universities are here is testament in part to the natural resources of the area of which Lake Merrit is a part. These resources that sustained our ancestors are now used in very different ways; bent, modified to our needs, and (in some ways) diminished.

Although the waterway no longer supplies much food, it now serves what is perhaps an even greater requirement for our society. As a place of respite, and open area where we can see the sky and look to other forms of life, Lake Merritt serves an inner need.

In Part II of this series, we will discuss the human history of Lake Merritt. But remember; man and his machines; his pumps that now control the water level are but a speck in time to the lake. She will be here when they are gone. For concrete and metal are unnatural, and therefore temporary. When we cease to maintain them (or when we cease to be) they will slowly deteriorate and crumble.

And slowly, through the eons, Lake Merritt will resume her intrinsic form, a slave to water, the tides, and the inherent laws that we may only temporarily direct for our own wellbeing.

43. THE LAKE IN THE YEARS SINCE CITYHOOD

January 18, 1994

Part one of this history series presented a brief description of what the land and water around Lake Merrit was like before the arrival of mankind. There is much from that period that we don't know, but the human history is more easily documented. Much of it is preserved on the second floor of the Oakland Public Library, and at the Cameron Stanford House, a Victorian-era embodiment of the fine culture that formerly graced much of the shoreline.

Our story begins when the land beneath the waters was known as San Antonio Creek, owned by Don Luis Peralta and part of the Rancho San Antonio. At this time the open body of water was much smaller, confined to what is now the center of lake Merritt, and surrounded by large mudflats. The tide flowed unobstructed and boats carrying commerce moved to and from San Francisco Bay. Don Luis named the tidal lagoon after himself, Lake Peralta.

In 1852 the city of Oakland was founded and a year later a toll bridge was built across San Antonio Creek to connect the new city with the village of Brooklyn. Shortly afterward, an imposing figure who was to play a significant part in the history of the lake arrived.

Dr. Samuel Merritt, who stood 6-foot 3 and weighed 340 pounds, had come west for the gold rush, and ultimately (together with two others) formed the Oakland Waterfront Company that controlled the entire shoreline.

By 1867 Merritt, whose booming voice preceded him into a room, had become mayor, and in 1869 a dam was built across the creek, enlarging the lake, and limiting tidal flow. Mayor Merritt then dedicated its waters as a "public lake." If this date is chosen as the birth of Lake Merritt, our urban estuary is 125 years sold this year. In 1870 the state governor sighed a bill establishing the area as the first wildlife refuge in North America. By the end of 1874 the name Lake Merritt had been used officially for the first time.

Then came the dark side. As more and more people came, pipes were installed and creeks became drains. Civilization brought toilets, and Lake Merritt became a harbor for the "necessities of nature." In 1884, 90 percent of the city's sewage flowed into the north arms of the Lake. By 1892 the City Engineer reported that the lake was filling in at the rate of one inch per year.

In response, Lake Merritt was dredged (apparently for the first time) in 1893, a project that continued more or less for the next 22 years and beyond. In 1907 the dredged material was used to fill in the mud flats around 12th Street. In 1922, the lake was dredged again and the material used to create the first of five bird islands in the refuge.

By the turn of the century, Lake Merritt had been branded a cesspool and a menace to public health. In 1912 the city passed an ordinance prohibiting swimming, a regulation that still exists today. Things had not improved much by the "Roaring Twenties," when the Fish and Game Commission called the lake "notoriously bad" and people were advised not to swim in the waters due to high bacterial levels. Lake Merritt was living on the edge; sustaining recreational boating and populations of fish, but succumbing to the periods when tidal action could not remove the massive load of pollutants carried in by the drains.

Along the shoreline however, things were looking up. In the progressive period after 1900 when major improvements were made to American cities, Mayor Frank Mott (not William Penn Mott) promoted improvements to the area. Between 1907 and 1925 these included the establishment of park lands, landscaping, wells, a fountain, the El Embarcadero columns, the municipal Boathouse, bandstand, lawn bowling greens, model yacht club, tennis courts, canoe house (now the sailboat house), a beach, a road around the lake and major buildings overlooking the waters.

After two temporary projects, the first in 1913, the "Necklace of Lights" became permanent in 1925 and soon appeared on postcards around the world. As this era came to a close, and the Great Depression began, Lake Merritt presented a paradox. Committed to it as a major park and recreation center, the city has not yet come to grips with the water pollution problems which would continue to grow as the population increased. Lake Merritt was serving as a recreation center, a wildlife refuge, a source of civic pride and proper tax enhancement, and unfortunately, the dumping grounds of sanitary and storm sewers.

In Part Three, we will learn how improvements in water quality were made, of the recent changes that created the environment we know today, and of the continuing battle against storm drain pollution.

44. DEVELOPMENT HAS GIVEN, TAKEN AWAY FROM THE LAKE

March 15, 1994

She turned the parasol to the far side of the boat, hiding the view of a dead rat drifting by. It was after all a lovely spring day on Lake Merritt. Despite the stock market crash, the water, wind, and sun still worked their magic, and a sense of peace pervaded the air, broken only by the cries of sea gulls overhead and children in the park. As the '30's began, the urban estuary was larger and more popular than it ever had been, but tidal flow was limited by the dam, and the sewer flow was increasing.

By 1930 a sailing club had been formed, and its regatta competed occasionally with outboard motor races and fishermen. Fish? Yes; despite the pollution after periods of rain, striped bass (imported from the east coast), salmon and other species entered the estuarine lake on incoming tides. In 1935 bass were so plentiful they were taken by pitchforks. But in 1939 over three tons of them perished in a massive fish kill, probably the result of low oxygen due to a neap tide and decomposition of organic matter from the storm drains and sewers.

Still, in 1948 the mayor's smelt derby began, a testimony to the resilience of the lake and its continuing biological productivity. Despite the pollution after periods of rain, the muted tides still flushed out waste and renewed the resource. On the shoreline, development continues. The Scottish Rite Temple was remodeled in art deco style by 1939 and the County Courthouse was built in the same period. By the 1950's Children's Fairyland had opened, enchanting the first children of the baby boom. Four more bird islands were built and the Rotary Science Center was completed in 1953. As the '60's progressed a cactus garden and public restaurant were completed.

Four years later the new museum opened nearby and in 1972 Estuary Park was completed, providing open space for nearby Laney College. The native Canadian geese saw their first "Festival at the Lake" in 1982, and in 1987 the necklace of lights was returned to its prior glory, having been abandoned after the bombing Pearl Harbor. Historians, however, do not appear to have recorded an equally important series of events.

Somewhere in this time period, the work of city engineers began to undo the wrongs they had created earlier. They began to connect the sewer pipes to waste water treatment plants, bypassing Lake Merritt. This work continued through the '80's, and the results were profound. Without its burden of waste water, Lake Merritt began to cleanse itself. A further drastic improvement came in 1985 when the entire Lake (except near the shoreline) was dredged, removing years of accumulated, polluted sediments.

As the 1990's began, water quality in Lake Merritt had improved to a point where body contact sports would be allowable based on summer bacterial counts. During the winter, when storm drains flush the streets into the Lake and large flocks of waterfowl defecate, bacterial levels exceed the standards. But when the rains end and most of the birds leave, levels of bacteria indicating pathogens decline and activities such as swimming, wading and wind surfing become perfectly safe.

Perception, however, lags behind change, and the "No Swimming" signs persist. I once met a man on the shore who declared that "there isn't a fish alive in this lake." Floating trash, the most obvious of the pollutants visible from the shoreline, reinforces this outdated image. True, the storm drains will dump their nasty burdens in the Lake, but with an average residence time of only four days before it is replaced, the water won't stay dirty.

The cleansing tides flush the lake, and the daily Clean-Up Crew snares what trash they can reach. Only in the sediments does the nasty stuff build up, spreading across the bottom until once again removed by dredging.

Lake Merritt is cleaner than at any other time in this century. The recent "Adapt A Storm Drain," "We Mean Clean," and county storm drain programs hold promise for an even cleaner watershed and estuary. Eventually, perhaps in the next century, the storm drains will be rerouted or channeled to upstream treatment basins, providing an even cleaner Lake

Merritt.   Nearby, the proposed Master Plan could restore the lands around the water, a fitting tribute to a unique, urban natural resource.

For now, though, we can reflect on several generations of how people have interacted with the waters we call Lake Merritt: Exploitation, expansion, development, pollution, recognition, improvement, and appreciation. As a new century dawns, one thing is certain. The lake will be here; how shall we relate to it?

45. GRANT ADVANCES LAKE MERRITT FOUNTAIN PROJECT

March 25, 1994

The concept of an aeration fountain to alleviate low oxygen conditions in part of Lake Merritt has received significant support in early 1994. In a great example of public/private partnership, volunteers and concerned citizens have taken three major steps toward realization of the enhancement.

First, through efforts of the East Bay Municipal Utilities District, an ITT Flygt pump will be donated to the city. Second, a public-spirited citizen has promised to construct a nozzle, or nozzles, which will direct the water spray into a desired pattern. Third, public support at a second public meeting in January confirmed that people want a fountain in Lake Merritt to provide aeration to the sometimes stagnant waters. With the awarding of a $2,500 grant by the Strong Foundation to the Lake Merritt Institute for the fountain, it now appears that only approval by Oakland's City Council is needed to bring the improvement to fruition.

At a Jan. 19 meeting of the city Environmental Affairs Commission, the technical aspects of aeration were discussed. Bubbler devices using air compressors (which can be noisy) inject compressed air at the Lake bottom. They are more likely to cause the release of hydrogen sulfide gas from the sediments than are water spray fountains. Upon realization that bubbler aeration devices are also limited in their efficiency by the minimal area for air/water contact, the group centered on discussion of a fountain. Information was provided by Dr. Alex Horne of UC-Berkeley's Engineering Department, and by a technical report completed for the Lake Merritt Resource Enhancement Plan.

Component parts of a fountain include a pump, pipes, nozzle(s), an electric power supply, and a water intake. Oxygen mixes with the water as it falls through the air and, cooled by evaporation, this aerated water sinks to the bottom where storm drain sediments are decomposing. In the presence of oxygen, this decomposition leads to carbon dioxide, useful in photosynthesis. But when oxygen is absent, smelly gasses such as hydrogen sulfide are produced. The fountain will not only increase oxygen levels in the water, but will also assist in preventing the buildup of anaerobic sediments, and thereby reduce the source of odors.

It should operate not only by day, but also at night when oxygen is not produced from photosynthesis.

Proposals have been made for a small fountain at El Embarcadero area (Grand and Lakeview) and a larger fountain at the end of Glen Echo Cove (Grand and Harrison). Plans for a small fountain at the El Embarcadero location inside the petro-barrier were chosen to go to the City Council for approval. Oxygen levels of near zero have often been measured at this site and the white columns and park-like ambience make it a good location for the aesthetics of falling waters. At present, the Environmental Affairs Commission has not yet scheduled the fountain proposal before the Council.

Remaining hurdles to overcome may include deciding if the fountains should be lighted and if so, finding lights; determining the most desirable spray pattern; and hooking the 230-volt 3.4 amp pump up to an inconspicuous junction box near the bulkhead. It should be possible to use the existing Lake Merritt Institute grant to cover electrical installation costs, and perhaps underwater lights can be donated as a tax deduction. A variety of spray patterns can be presented to the Council for their review when approval is considered.

With continued support, the fountain could be installed and working in time for this year's Festival of the Lake, an appropriate forum to showcase the city's support for water quality and Lake Merritt.

Note: As many as four locations had fountains in recent years, but changing water levels and siltation rendered them inoperable.

46. LAKE MERRITT IMPROVEMENTS RIDE ON THE JUNE BALLOT

April 19, 1994

June, 1994 will be a pivotal time for the future of Lake Merritt. In one 24-hour period, voters in California will embrace or reject a proposition called CALPAW: the California Wildlife, Coastal and Parks Initiative. Embedded in its language is a paragraph pertaining to Lake Merritt and promising $10 million for certain kinds of enhancement, improvement, and parkland expansion. Ten million dollars. It sounds like a lot of money. But, given the opportunities, and the problems, is it really?

Consider the opportunities. A parkland corridor over 12th Street, connecting Lakeside Park to Estuary Park and the Bay Trail; removal of the polluted storm-drain sediments for the first time since 1985; a vegetative master plan with native plants and blossoming trees; and re-creation of small salt marsh habitats to restore a portion of lost diversity and all the living things that a marsh brings. Add to that replacement of the crumbling bulkheads with a more natural shoreline and 10 million begins to look like not enough.

But not enough will not even exist if voters like you and me don't support CALPAW. The campaign to raise funds for its passage, and for Oakland to receive its share, has begun. Non-tax-deductible contributions may be made payable to CALPAW '94 and sent to: 926 J St., Suite 612, Sacramento, CA 95814. For further information contact Jerry Meral, campaign director at the league.

Even if you are not a fan of Lake Merritt, there are plenty of other reasons to vote yes on this initiative. State parks, wildlife habitat and coastal protection projects will all benefit. These include almost 400 specific areas that have been designated for purchase and protection. Trails, archaeological/historic resources, and recreational facilities throughout the state will all benefit.

Considering California's growth in population, we need this.

Local conservation leaders have worked hard to insert Lake Merritt funds into the initiative. The fact that such a sum of money is singled out for our unique urban estuary is testimony to the importance of Lake Merritt not only to Oakland, but also to the region, and to the entire state.

There is a group of people, however that doesn't want the initiative to pass. They wear black hoods, dress in T-shirts with evil words and carry tools of destruction. They are known as the Raiders of the Last Park: Greed, Ignorance, Self-interest, and Apathy. Beware of them for they sacrifice the future for the present; the value of many for the demands of the few; and the last vestiges of the natural world for concrete and sterility. Should economic fears and Raiders prevail, Lake Merritt will still exist. But the opportunities to grow and become something even more useful, beautiful, and outstanding will be lost.

Beyond the tangible resources of land and structures, passage of the initiative will promote those things that go deeper; pride, satisfaction, and community.

There is an opportunity here. An opportunity to say "We Care." If you agree, help fund the CALPAW Victory Fund; and next June when the young ducks catch their first fish from the Lake, vote yes.

47. CONTRIBUTE TO THE FUTURE OF LAKE MERRITT

April 22, 1994

Come back, Samuel Merritt: We still need you. We need your spirit, dedication, and vision. We need the ambition and strength that you used to bring a renewable natural resource into the midst of a great city. Unfortunately, the former mayor after whom the Lake is named cannot come back from the dead, but that doesn't mean his work is finished.

As the end of the century approaches, as the tide continues to ebb and flow into the city, and as Oakland struggles to recapture its former brilliance, we need someone to pick where Dr. Merritt left off. We need a period of civic pride; a period of restoration, enhancement, and progression. Much of what makes Lake Merritt great was created in such a period, as were many of the classical components of Central Park in New York, Golden Gate Park in San Francisco, and Lincoln Park in Chicago. These and other examples of civic enrichment continue to nourish our lives today.

So profound and lasting were these improvements that they have touched several generations, and will continue to provide inspiration for decades to come. It is time for another such period, another time of glory, and another such leader.

It has been said that periods of social change and growth come in cycles. A civil war in the 1860's, the gay '90's, the roaring '20's and the times that changed in the 1960's are certainly examples. The intervening time between these periods has been 30-40 years, and they have occurred at least four times in the last two centuries.

If this theory is true, the 1990's could be part of this cycle. The '90's are now, and if such a period is about to begin, it should well include lake Merritt. Perhaps what is needed to start such an era for the Lake is a benefactor. What could such a benefactor (individual or corporation) accomplish? For starters, how about implementation of a Master Plan for the Lake and Lakeside Park. Details? How about statues of Jack London, of Sam Merritt, of Gertrude Stein and of William Penn Mott? How about a beautiful ring of natural and flowering vegetation around the shoreline to complement the necklace of lights; an endowment for periodic dredging and other water quality improvements?

How about expansion of the parkland and creation of mini-wetlands along the shoreline; restoration of the dilapidated piers and an aeration fountain worthy of the century plus that Lake Merritt has served Oakland? With these and other improvements, the natural and human resource values of Lake Merritt could soar into the twentieth century. The enrichment would be not only for the people of Oakland, but also for the benefactor. Included in the laurels would be a place in history, the realization that comes from knowing you have made a permanent change in both an urban and natural ecosystem. The sponsor of such projects would realize both personal gratification and, if wanted, public acknowledgment. If such rewards appeal to you, step forward, contribute and be recognized.

There are several ways to contribute to the future of Lake Merritt and Oakland. Participation in the Lake Merritt Institute or Lake Merritt Breakfast Club is certainly an option. For those with more financial resources than time, specific donations for identified projects are a good opportunity. There is certainly no lack of worthy projects; a stroll through the park and a vision of what could be will easily bring many to mind. Combine that with a little homework, dedication and consensus building, and history could be changed.

Samuel Merritt did it; and now it is our turn. But none of us are getting any younger, and today's opportunities can easily grow cold. The place is here, and the time is now. Who will be the next Samual Merritt?

Note: See the back cover for ways you can help Lake Merritt.

48. CLEANING AGENTS ARE BAD NEWS FOR WATER QUALITY

May 6, 1994

You can see the telltale ring around the storm drain grates: A grayish-white stain of phosphates, surfactants, grease, and grime. They also appear behind the pet shop, the restaurant, and the grocery store. Although unnoticed by almost everyone, they mark the locations of a significant source of pollution to Lake Merritt; mop bucket water.

Daily the workers pour their concoctions of detergent, Pine Sol, Spic and Span and floor wax into the pipes. Under orders from management, trained by supervisors and assisted by co-workers, they dutifully pollute Lake Merritt by pouring their dirty water into the storm drains.

These pipes (as those of you who read this column know by now) drain directly into the downtown urban estuary: Not to treatment plant, not to the Bay, but straight to our recreational lake. After a brief flow downhill, this polluted water emerges from the big six and seven foot diameter storm drains at Lakeside and Grand, from the four foot drain along Harrison Street, and from the dozens of other storm drains that ring the lake.

The visible part is a floating scum. The invisible part (dissolved salts and other chemicals) emerges within the water. Both components spread throughout the 160 acres, confusing wildlife, degrading property values, and concentrating in the sediments. No one knows how much of this stuff enters the lake, or what the real effects are on mussels, fish, and waterfowl. Concentrations vary by season and rainfall event.

Dumped on a day of limited tidal influence and slow storm drain flows, the soapy mess can easily contaminate a large area of the lake, violating unenforced water quality criteria and contributing to the "bad image" of Lake Merritt and Oakland. The absence of encrusting organisms near the storm drain outlets may be from fresh water, or from pollution, and one can't avoid being disgusted by the residues that we instinctively know don't belong there.

Who is responsible? If you are a shopkeeper in the area that drains to Lake Merritt (much of Piedmont, downtown and west Oakland), the bell tolls for you. If you are a mop bucket dumper or someone responsible for where the dumpers dump, you could be polluting the lake, and could be subject to enforcement action. Legalities aside, we're all in this together; it's our city and our loss in property values, water quality and environment.

The solution is not difficult: When finished mopping, pour the water down the toilet. From there the pipe leads to a wastewater treatment plant, designed to remove the soap, nutrients, and most other chemicals. Like most things that sound easy, it is not. To be effective, the message must reach hundreds of people, a difficult task at best.

How best to communicate this message? We have already labeled many of the storm drains (which has definitively helped), but many are probably hidden from view in back alleys and on private property.

One could pass a law, but a Mop Bucket Disposal Act of 1994 would probably not compete well with redevelopment proposals or budget items for the Council's time. Still, a proclamation would generate publicity, and that is what is needed. In the final analysis, public consciousness is raised by the media. Channel Two: Are you out there? Oakland Tribune: Do you care enough about Oakland to dig into the story? If drama is needed, I'll even volunteer to be arrested on camera while "polluting" the storm drain with colored water. The sight of an arresting officer and of the murky mixture emerging from the pipe into the lake will be effective. A few minutes on the airwaves and a few square inches in newsprint could do wonders to keep Lake Merritt clean.

Interested parties may contact the Lake Merritt Institute at 238-7104.

49. SUMMER BRINGS WINDSURFERS TO LAKE MERRITT

July 15, 1994

A new era will soon begin at Lake Merritt when windsurfing comes to the estuary. The popular sport has been approved beginning this summer, a time when levels of bacteria in the water remain consistently below the criteria for body contact. The colorful, speedy triangular sails have never been seen on the lake before, but are likely to become a common sight given the popularity of the sport and the suitability of Samuel Merritt's Lake for such activity.

Almost since its formation, swimming and other body contact sports have been discouraged or prohibited at the lake due to pollution from storm and sanitary sewers. But times have changed and (except on a rare occasion in the winter when heavy rainfall and ground water infiltration fill up the sanitary sewers, causing them to overflow into the storm sewer) sewage does not enter the lake. Storm water still flows in, but only during the rainy season. In the summer, only the tides enter the Lake, flushing it with cleaner water from San Francisco Bay and the Pacific.

Yes, there was a recent sewage leak reported in the media; but no, that doesn't mean the water is still polluted. Given the fact that the entire volume of water in Lake Merritt is flushed every four days (more often when the tides are high, less when they are low) the diluted wastewater is quickly dispersed.

In addition, the estuary is a biological system, and well suited to modifying foreign life forms (such as pathogenic bacteria). Pathogens are pathogens because they infect the human body. As such, they like stable, warm conditions. Expose them to sunlight, salty water, competing bacteria , cold, silt, algae etc. and they die. A major sewage spill in 1989, much larger than our recent one, was flushed out in less than one week, and bacterial readings were back to normal.

How do we know that Lake Merritt is safe enough for a body contact sport such as windsurfing? Basically, we measure bacteria, that part of pollution that has the potential for causing disease. But not just any bacteria. Many of these single celled organisms are beneficial, incapable of causing disease and common in the environment. So, we measure an indicator organism, one which is known to exist along with pathogenic bacteria, which are organisms that can cause illness.

For water quality, the most common bacteria that indicate the potential presence of disease causing organisms are a group called fecal coliforms. These types of "bugs" as microbiologists call them, are found in large numbers within fecal matter; and it doesn't matter if it's from a dog, human, cow, bird etc. In fact, birds, especially water fowl, have one of the highest concentrations of fecal coliform bacteria per gram of feces of any animal known. They are a significant source of fecal coliform bacteria in Lake Merritt. But not all fecal coliforms cause disease: if they did, their common distribution would mean disaster for us all.

Through extensive and convincing research, levels of fecal coliform bacteria have been determined that are safe, border-line, and not safe. At not-safe levels, the really bad bugs (real pathogens) exist in numbers large enough to make us sick. In water environment such as Lake Merritt, sick typically means digestive disorders, rashes, and inflammation of the mucous membranes; which are generally not life threatening diseases

True, Typhoid, and other killers can be carried in water, but they generally occur only when you drink water from conditions that are really polluted. You would know that such water was not for drinking or swimming.

Beginning in 1990, under contract with the Alameda County Flood Control and Water Conservation District, a consulting firm has sampled the water in Lake Merritt for bacteria every two to five weeks. The results of this sampling have provided the basis for determining that Lake Merritt is safe for water contact during the summer months (see the Montclarion issue of March 24, 1992). Body contact is deemed safe (i.e. you won't get sick) when fecal coliform levels are below 1,000 colony forming units per 100 milliliters of water (CFU/100ml).

From 1991 to 1992, fecal coliform levels at central Lake Merritt ranged from 4 to 510 during June, July and August, and most values were below 254. It is in the central area of the Lake that tidal flushing is greatest, and bacterial counts are lowest. At the swim beaches (near Children's Fairy-land and the inlet/outlet channel) counts were usually somewhat higher, but still well below the level that would be declared too high.

So wax up your board and get out the bathing suit. Given a typical brisk late afternoon breeze, you'll soon be able to blow by the racing sculls which will be no match for the windsurfers in terms of knots. And, the Sail Boat House staff (assuming they are not eliminated by budget cuts) will even be offering lessons.

Note: See the recent article on swimming in Lake Merritt in the "Oaklandside" on August 23, 2023

50. THE JOURNEY OF A WATER DROP: LAKE MERRITT AND BEYOND

September 2, 1994

Although fictitious, the following account of Lake Merritt's hydrology is based on fact. Well, fact if you consider the computer model devised by Phil Williams and Associates to be reality.

In 1992, as part of the Resource Enhancement Plan, the hydrology of Lake Merritt was examined in detail and entered in a mathematical model combining equations for tidal movements and stormwater runoff. The model has been used for several purposes, including determination of what types of marsh plants will grow in the lake, how long water remains in our urban estuary, and predicting high and low water levels over a typical cycle. Essential information; useful too, but pretty dry stuff unless you're a hydrological engineer. But if we can imagine what life is like for a drop of water...

Born as molecules condensed from vapor high over the Pacific and carried by the westerlies to coastal mountains, the droplets of water drifted in the wind. Falling, dropping from the sky miles above the metropolis, they created rain. Many fell onto the earth. Some were pulled back into plants, transpired back into vapor, and re-entered the atmosphere. Some fell onto rooftops, sidewalks and the streets of Oakland and Piedmont.

Furiously they responded to gravity in a relentless movement ever downward. If there is a single law that governs water, it is gravity. Until, that is, it reaches the sea. There the tidal forces (a form of gravity exerted by the moon and sun) take over.

It was dark and cold in the pipe. The journey over pavement and street had been fast and furious as the drops merged into one flow, sweeping all that floated or dissolved along with it. Now the storm drain pipe was nearly full.

But the water was no longer pure, having been mixed with the oily film of the street, traces of fertilizer from the over-fed lawns, paper, cigarette butts and plastic, hydrocarbons from auto exhausts and trace of metal from industry. A bubbly scum floated at the top. Heavy particles of sand and soil moved more slowly along the bottom. Finally, in a gush like hitting the bottom of a water slide, what had been rain and was now runoff, entered Lake Merritt.

Movement rapidly slowed. Sediment dropped out, first the sand, then lighter particles and silt, joining a growing mound of other mud on the lake bottom. Freed of its burden and confinement in the pipe, our drop of water swirled out into the open lake, fresh water floating atop a saltier and heavier layer of water below that had entered the lake as tidal flow. Gradually, the movement stopped, leaving the water bobbing in the waves and re-absorbing oxygen that had been lost to chemicals in the pipe. Sunlight penetrated the drop, and duck kicked it while diving after a fish.

By now the lake was "full," meaning that at an elevation of 2.8 feet above the National Geodetic Vertical Datum (NGVD) had been reached. Above this height, at 3.0 feet and above, flooding of adjacent streets would occur as had happened in the 1950's.

Beyond the tidal gates separating the lake from San Francisco Bay, the tide had dropped six feet, and the water level was now lower than that of the Lake. The gates were opened, and for the next several hours, Lake Merritt emptied its load of rain water into the larger estuary. Then, as the tide rose and blocked the lake's outflow, flood control pumps were turned on, reversing the normal tidal flow as Lake Merritt continued to drain. That the Bay rises and falls more than six feet while Lake Merritt's level changes no more than 2.5 feet is due to the limited volume of water that can pass through the narrow, shallow inlet/outlet channel.

For three days the drop of water remained in the lake. Four days is the average residence time for any drop of water in Lake Merritt, but heavy rains and high tides had swelled the currents and quickened the pulse of circulation. Without the rain, and during more limited tides, our drop might remain for five or more days. Eventually though, calculations indicate that all water is returned to the larger bay, and thence to the ocean from whence it came. The tidal prism (volume of water exchanged each day between the higher high and lower low tides) under the normal, continuously open, operation of the tide gates is about 150 – 200 acre feet, and this occurs in about 12 hours. The volume of the of Lake itself varies with the tidal level, but is about 1,200 acre feet.

Someday someone will conduct an "in the field" circulation study, releasing numbered oranges (biodegradable and organic) at the inlet and lemons at the storm drains, and track their journey around the lake. Then we will know (at least for the surface water) the real comings and goings of Lake Merritt water. Until then, we must be content with computer calculations.

It had been a useful journey for the water droplet. During its time in Lake Merritt, it had passed through the gills of a topsmelt, brought oxygen to the tiny fish; supported a racing scull in its own journey across the lake; and reflected the sunset over thousands of windows overlooking the water. It had lapped the mussel laden piers of an abandoned dock, carried plankton into a clam, and cooled the hot afternoon air downtown.

Back in the ocean and salty again, life was less complicated. There just wasn't that much to do. Its journey, however, has been predicted by a computer model, and when it returns, we will know what to expect.

51. EVERYONE CAN ENJOY THE BEAUTY OF LAKE MERRITT

November 11, 1994

Both man and master in the night are one. All things are equal when the day is done.

The prince and the plowman, the slave and the freeman. All find their comfort in old John O 'Dreams.

These words, from the Irish song "John O 'Dreams," were written by Bill Caddick ©. They convey the age-old message that even though our day's work may segregate us into classes of status and station, we are, after all, one people. We are reminded of this daily when, our work done, we all must sleep. The dreams and solitude of these hours are ours, not our masters; and though the bed may be rags or feathers, this peace may not be disturbed.

Now as you sleep the dreams come with you. The hawks of morning cannot harm you here.

Sleep is a river, flows on forever. And for your boatman choose old John O 'Dreams.

Both man and master are equal when the day is done. Regardless of what we do by day to pay the bills, night comes to us all in the same way, and we respond equally. The stars shine the same, and the moonlight is there for all to ponder. The night is a time of equality for all people.

But by day, under the harsh light of the sun and scrutiny of society, is there a place that accepts man and master as one? Is there somewhere we can go to rest without the signs "Private Property" or "No Loitering" to differentiate between the haves and have nots? Where is there such a place that does not discriminate, where peace is offered equally to all those open to accept it?

Such a place is Lake Merritt. The open water, distant vistas and timeless tides are free to all; they exist in isolation from our civilization and her rankings, from our jobs and time clocks, and the geese don't care if you're Black or White, Asian, or Hispanic, rich, or poor. Lay down on the green grass, gaze up at the blue sky, and let the stillness flow over you. Close your eyes and listen to the water lap along the shore. It will still be there when you wake up, and in a year, and in a decade, and in a century. You can come back every day. You can watch the children and young fish, and stay until the night heron wings away at dusk.

Across the hills the sun has gone its way. Tomorrow's cares are many dreams away.

The stars are flying, your candle's dying. Yield now the nighttime to old John O ' Dreams.

Lake Merritt belongs to all people, and to no one. We do not control the movements of the water or the creatures that live there. And it does not control us. That such a place exists without prejudice is perhaps the meaning of a natural resource, as opposed to one created by mankind. We did not create it; and it does not judge us.

This is conceivably the greatest value of Lake Merritt, and her greatest lesson.

In the melting pot that is Oakland there exists a resource of which we all may partake equally. That is there for man and master, that flows on forever, and that offers its beauty for all of us. What more can we ask?

52. MARSHES ARE A LAKE MERRITT PRIORITY

December 16, 1994

Salt water marshes formerly flourished in the coves and shallows of Lake Merritt. Long before the dam restricted tidal flow, before the bulkheads created artificial shorelines and before dredging destroyed the mudflats, pickleweed and gum plant, salt grass and *Atriplex* all grew at the water's edge. There were more waterfowl then, and a greater variety of plants and animals. Alternately flooded and exposed by tides, the marshes took nutrients from the water and returned them as food to the ecosystem.

Remnants exist: Bits and pieces along the inlet-outlet channel and among the crumbling rock of the older bulkheads. Along one of the few natural shorelines at the north side of the peninsula where bulkheads do not exist, one can still see a few of these plants growing. Their presence indicates that, at certain tidal elevations, conditions are right for their growth.

This conclusion was verified in the Lake Merritt Resource Enhancement Plan completed in 1992. Computer modeling of tidal flows demonstrated that the observed tidal range (verified by 24-hour tide gauges at the Rowboat House and Pump Station) matches the known requirements of what is known as the "High Salt Marsh" assemblage of plants and animals. Where these conditions exist elsewhere in the Bay Area, a high salt marsh grows.

Such a marsh does not include the tall cord grass (*Spartina*) stands that one associates with the low saltmarsh. This plant requires higher tidal variations than exist in Lake Merritt. But for the plants that typically grow landward of cordgrass, conditions at our urban estuary are favorable.

Because such a marsh would restore some of the lost biological and visual diversity, protect currently eroding areas, and be beneficial to wildlife, the Enhancement Plan made creation of four small (less than three acres) marsh areas the number 4 priority recommendation. Creation of marsh areas was also the number 2 priority of 19 Lake Merritt improvement projects voted on at a December public meeting. Clearly, there is public support for this idea.

This support lives with Karen Orso. A member of the California Native Plant Society and botanist by avocation, she has been collecting seeds from the remnant high marsh plants in Lake Merritt since 1993. The seeds have sprouted, and produced plants that would be invaluable for use in recreating the lake's lost marshlands. Ms. Orso wrote me a while back and offered to help; a gracious offer that should not be turned down.

In addition, the Lake Merritt Institute is interested in the proposed wetland restoration. Although not official policy, this project may be next on the list after the fountain is successfully up and running (due in a few months). So, we have a recommendation in a study supported by the City Office of Parks and Recreation, seeds, and plants, Institute interest and public support.

Why aren't the marsh areas under construction? In an attempt to put a complicated process simply, the following (at least) are needed: 1) A construction plan with cost estimate; 2) Approval of that plan by the Office of Parks and Recreation, the Park and Recreation Advisory Commission, the Boating Advisory Board, the Landmarks Preservation Board, the Rotary Science Center Advisory Board, and the City Office of Public Works; 3) A form 302 signed by all city departments; 4) Funding to pay for it; 5) Approval by the City Council Cultural services and Public Works Subcommittees; 6) Approval by the full City Council; and 7) A successful bid to do the work. Oh, and a lack of opposition. Our system seems designed to facilitate opposition, no matter what its cause or rationale.

How then, and when, will the marshland recommendation become a reality? What is needed is the dedication of an individual to guide the process; someone to work with all the above groups to attend meetings, to lobby and to advocate. Can the process work without such a leader? Perhaps, but much slower. Also needed is an engineering plan with details on the amount of soil needed, site boundaries and costs.

The salary isn't very enticing (zero unless we can find a grant to include paying a project manager), but the experience would look great on a resume or when one approaches the "Pearly Gates." Most of all, there would be the satisfaction when the job was done in knowing that it was worthwhile. So, engineers and marsh managers, step forward. History awaits you.

Note: Small, high marshes have been planted at the Boating Center and along the channel, but vandalism plagues the latter.

53. MERMAID TALES OF OAKLAND'S JEWEL

January 10, 1995

Darkness seemed to come early to the lake. Only a single rowing shell with its bright green bow light could be seen out on the water. Along the Lakeside Park peninsula, strong waves washed into the eroding shoreline. It was cold.

Miska, the mermaid who lived in Lake Merritt, was very sad. The new year had come, but the lake was dark and empty. There were no other animals around, and no one who seemed to care about her. She was lonely, and a little bit afraid. It wasn't just that the winter rains had washed away her favorite algae, for mermaids really don't need to eat. As a life form that is continually being reborn in people's minds, she lived on more than just simple food, and was really kept alive as a tradition nurtured by those who believed in her.

She swam to where sea gulls often perch on the broken dock in front of the Lake Merritt Hotel. The structure, no longer connected to the shoreline, made her even more depressed. There she met here friend Jonathan the sea gull, recently arrived from Orange County where life for even a sea gull was difficult these days.

"Things are not really going very well," she complained to Jonathan. "The good Mr. Kaufmann, ranger at the Rotary Science Center, has left, and it appears that a full-time replacement may not be hired. Now Stephanie may have to teach the children's classes and feed the birds alone. Even the lights on the floating Christmas tree are gone, another victim of the city's financial difficulties." And, she added, "the lake keeps getting shallower, filled in with silt, leaves and debris washed in from the winter rains. When will they ever dredge it again?"

Jonathan sighed and agreed that the lake definitely has its problems. "Our potential is nowhere near being met" he said; "what with the odors, limited wildlife habitat and reduced city funding, the jewel of Oakland seems a bit tarnished sometimes."

A loud splash interrupted their talk. "That was no fish," said Miska. There followed a muffled cry for help out in the lake from where the boat had been. Quickly, they swam to the center where it is nine feet deep at high tide. When they got there, it wasn't a human, it was a spirit!

"Who are you?" Shouted Miska.

"I, ... I am the spirit of Oakland," came the reply. "But I can't go on. I'm drowning."

"But you must live," cried Jonathan, "we need you. Everyone needs you."

"You don't understand," said the spirit.

"Yes, I do," replied Miska. "You can do more than you think. Just try; you don't know what will happen. After all, life is what happens to us while we're making other plans. But if you don't try, nothing will happen. Don't give in to the dark waters."

It was no use. The spirit of Oakland slipped under the waters of Lake Merritt and vanished. Miska dived down and with a mighty flip of her tail, pushed the spirit back to the surface. "Now you listen to me," she said. "I've seen worse times than these in this city, and I know that together we can make it better. But you've got to try; I can't push you all the way to the dock alone." Slowly the spirit began to swim, and as it neared the shoreline, the necklace of lights came on, sparkling across the water. The lights reminded the spirit of what it had done, and of what it could do.

"Yes, I will try," it said. "I won't give up."

"We'll help" shouted Miska and Jonathan. "And we'll get our friends to help too."

And so the spirit of Oakland lived, as it lives today. It is out there, trying; trying to make a better Lake Merritt, a better city, and a better people. If you believe in Miska, and in the spirit, you can help. You just have to try.

Note: This dock was rebuilt with funds raised by the Lake Committee of the Lake Merritt Breakfast Club.

54. CANADIAN GEESE FIND SANCTUARY ALONG LAKE MERRITT'S SHORES

January 27, 1995

Wings Across the Freeways

It is early evening and you are driving south on 880 past Jack London Square. A golden hue to the west over San Francisco anticipates the twilight, while traffic slows to a standstill as yet another human mishap disturbs the unnatural order. With the window down to catch the cool wind, you hear it – a distant call.

Then, about 30 feet overhead, they appear: A formation of six Canadian geese winging their way back to Lake Merritt for the night's shelter. Unobstructed, they glide over the stalled vehicles below to the open water and darkened trees ahead. Having sought sustenance along the Bay shoreline, they are returning home to join the flock. A while later, in the darkening gloom, a larger silhouette flies overhead. A night heron, having slept by day, begins a night of feasting.

These birds live at Lake Merritt and owe their existence to the open waters, islands, and protection there. But their influence covers a wider area. Being airborne, they can and do move across Oakland, reminding others in places away from the Lake that we share this planet with other living things.

The sight of them reminds us that there is another type of existence. An older, more simple world with its own separate and inherent order. Without Lake Merritt, we would not have this reminder. So, the next time you are driving down 880 at sunset, look skyward; and remember, we are not alone.

Tubeworms in the Tires

They're still there. Little white tubeworms called *Mercierella* used to thickly cover much of the hard substrate at Lake Merritt, but disappeared in the early '90s (see The Montclarion, Dec. 7, 1993). They can, however, still be found in a sheltered location at piers along the shoreline. They exist within tires bolted to the dock for protection of boats. In small numbers, perhaps, but exist they do.

Here they find refuge from competing Asian clams which (perhaps) cannot attach to the steel-belted radial tires. Critters usually find a way to survive; much like the dinosaurs in Jurassic Park that were not supposed to be able to breed, but did. Our lowly tubeworm at Lake Merritt provides a parallel to the movie's message. Nature finds a way.

Connect the Parks

Have you ever tried to walk from Lake Merritt to Estuary Park? You can't. If you try to follow the channel, a fence blocks the way; forcing a detour along uninviting streets away from the water. This obstruction between two remnants of Oakland's natural waterfront has not gone unnoticed. Soon (by bureaucratic standards) a trail will ring San Francisco Bay, providing hikers, bikers, strollers, joggers, and tots in buggies a path from which to traverse the waterfront. Many believe it should be connected to Lake Merritt, and not just a hole in the fence.

Watch this column for further news of plans for a "connector trail" or a Lid Park" over 12th Street: a fitting and appropriate isle of green to connect Lake Merritt and the Convention Center. The waterfowl may be able to wing over it freely, but we mere mortals need a little help.

55. LAKE MERRITT NEEDS MORE THAN SINGLE DAY OF PUBLIC ATTENTION, CARE

June 9, 1995

I bought a record back in the '60s called "God Bless the Grass" by Pete Seeger. Along with songs of the times about how grass overpowers concrete, the beauty of the American landscape, and how small the earth looks from afar, there is a song by Malvina Reynolds and Pete Seeger called "70 Miles." It tells of San Francisco Bay back in the days before the Bay Commission put a stop to filling the Bay for such things as housing and garbage dumps. Although it was not written about Lake Merritt, one could change a few words around and it would describe what our Lake was like 30 years ago before recent improvements. Doing so, it might sound like this:

> What's that stinky Lake out there, out behind the high-rise back stairs?
>
> Sludgy bottom, sad and gray, why man, that's Lake Merritt Bay.
>
> 160 acres of wind and spray, 160 acres of water. 160 acres of open bay, it's a storm drain dump.
>
> Storm drains here, storm drains there; docks and tidelands disappear.
>
> Festering algae on the shallow ground, the dredge is nowhere to be found.
>
> Dump our garbage in the street; some folks think, "Gee, that's neat."
>
> When cries of anger fill the air, they'll just say, "I don't care.

Lake Merritt has, of course, improved immensely since the 1960s. Removal of sewage flow and years of accumulated sediment were the main improvements, but there remain dilapidated docks and areas of crumbling shoreline. Somehow, the lessons of the 1960s have faded as the '80s and '90s budget cuts took their toll.

Missing, too, is the collective call to action to remedy the ill. Demonstrate for Lake Merritt? Perhaps, but probably in the form of an Earth Day or anniversary event where thousands join hands around the Lake to show their support for a clean environment. Stay tuned; it could happen.

Many would like to see Earth Day clean-up events concentrated at Lake Merritt, the coming together of hundreds of volunteers to remove a winter's accumulation of storm drain trash, celebrate common values and the renewal of spring.

Also, watch for Lake Anniversary celebrations this year sponsored by the Merritt Lakesiders and the Rotary Nature Science Center. Lake Merritt would be an appropriate setting for such events; a natural world melded with a metropolis. Who knows, maybe Pete Seeger would come and sing to us.

God bless the grass, and God bless Lake Merritt.

56. EDUCATIONAL OPPORTUNITIES AT THE LAKE

June 20, 1995

Among the changes occurring in education today is a trend toward a holistic approach to learning. Using a single theme (such as The Oceans) to teach many of the traditional disciplines such as biology, mathematics, history, reading and writing not only enhances student interest, but also provides a real-world example to which they can relate.

In such a classroom, students would perhaps read how a lack of fresh water hindered early ocean exploration, experiment with hatching brine shrimp in waters of different salinities, and write about why the ocean is salty. By interconnecting the study skills they will need in life with a common theme, learning is more effective, more fun, and more useful.

It also helps to have a real place to study. A living laboratory with real animals, things to measure, and something that stimulates all six senses (well five maybe). Such a place is Lake Merritt. As an educational resource, consider the following:

- Past studies have developed a wealth of information to use in teaching
- Classrooms exist at the Rotary Science Center, Junior Center of Art & Science and Sailboat House
- As a "mini-ocean" Lake Merritt embodies many of the life forms, physical phenomena and cyclical processes that exist in seas around the world
- As an urban estuary, the lake provides us with a place to study the interaction of people with a natural resource
- Society's pollution problems can be studied, as can the history of human impact that first degraded and exploited, and now attempts to restore
- It is accessible: As near as Grand and Lakeshore; three feet from the sidewalk.

Given these attributes, what can be done to use the educational opportunities of the lake? With city budgets dwindling and the demand for necessary services increasing, taxpayer money is in short supply. For those that can afford it, classes for a fee are a viable option. For the less affluent, and for equipment and supplies needed to teach, we must look to grants from foundations, and contributions from local businesses.

Grant applications have been and are being written. There is talk of establishing a high school and college program in environmental restoration to be based at the lake. The Lake Merritt Institute has submitted a proposal to develop and teach three elementary school classes to be taught at and on the waters of Lake Merritt. Could it happen here? Could an educational program be developed to teach students from Oakland and nearby East Bay communities?

It depends on us: You and I. Goethe knew this when he said:

> "Whatever you will or dream you can; begin it. Boldness has genius, power, and magic in it."

Why teach our youth? If we are to survive as a civilization, we must. In the beginning when people were few and food, shelter and warmth were scarce, life was more expendable. As we developed control over the world's resources, access to wealth, security, and abundance were possible. Today, as natural resources such as fertile land, minerals, clean water, and forests diminish, we can no longer look to them to sustain us all. There are too many of us.

The answer to providing opportunities for today's population lies not in resource exploitation of the past, but in utilization of knowledge and technology to obtain the currency to meet our needs.

An unskilled, hungry person cares less about his neighbor, or his property. A person knowledgeable enough to earn a decent wage is a good citizen. Knowledge from resources, not their exploitation, is the key to the future.

Note: Educational programs are offered by the Lake Merritt Institute, Junior Center, and Rotary Science Center.

57. A SHIPWRECK AT THE BOTTOM OF THE LAKE?

August 8, 1995

It happened a long time ago, said the storyteller. Long before the time of Samuel Merritt; long before the channel to the Bay was dammed (damned)? when ships passed freely between what was to become Lake Merritt and the sea beyond. There had been a small barge that carried supplies inland to the village and, although there are no pictures of her, she probably was more like the Lake Merritt King, a research barge of a scow now used for sample collecting, Halloween islands and (formerly) Christmas trees.

"Wake up son, you're falling overboard."

"Gee, I was dreaming about old boats" he said, rubbing his eyes.

"Well, be careful," I said, "or you'll join the ones on the bottom."

"What, a wreck on the bottom?" His eyes lit up.

"No one knows what's down there," I told him, "but during the Silt Study Depth Survey there were some strange blips on the sonar."

The depth transects had indeed shown some previously unreported features below the waters. For example, the inlet/outlet channel has a scour trough about 100 feet wide, with a bottom of washed shell and fine sand, not the black, oozy mud that predominates elsewhere. It is 10 feet deeper than the adjacent shallow areas, and often the site of wheeling waterfowl which feed on the schools of topsmelt. Fishermen know it as a great spot to try for striped bass too. The depth gradually tapers off out in the lake, and the underwater gully finally disappears when it is 40 feet wide at about 250 feet from the bridge.

There is also a big V-8 engine block down there I'm told, sunk after the wreck of a racing boat. That was back in the days when national speed boat racing was a big sport on Lake Merritt. It's hard to believe now, when motors are used only by the city staff on the 160 acre aquatic preserve, but the snarling sounds of little muffled infernal combustion engines once tore across the waters, devouring peace and sanity in their wake. No wonder the mermaids left! Doubtless the Merritt Lakesiders didn't like it either as the roar echoed into the adjoining residences overlooking the lake. Thank you, city, for ending the madness.

"Were pirate ships sunk here, too?" said the little girl.

"Go back to sleep" I replied. And she did. A jolly roger fluttered in her dreams.

"Avast, man the grappling hooks," shouted a bearded, bandana-headed figure on a pirate boat. The little barge that had sought shelter from the gale was no match for the swifter pirate ship as she came about, trapped in the narrow, northeastern channel that is now Glen Echo cove. Then, just as the cannon was lit, the pirate ship ran aground (the lake needed dredging back then too!) causing the gun to lurch starboard and sending the shot harmlessly ashore. Deer scattered at the noise. She was hopelessly stuck as the tide rapidly dropped, and the wind and waves did the rest, sinking the vessel offshore of today's Lake Merritt Hotel. Is that the strange echo on the depth chart today?

Perhaps we'll never really know, at least until divers explore it one day. Was it a dream, or did pirates once sail in Oakland? Is there plunder and booty buried in the sediment, or was it sucked up by the dredges that deepened the lake in the many decades since?

One hundred and sixty acres of downtown real estate that no one has ever seen. But there are blips on the sonar. What is down there?

58. A LOOK INTO THE LAKE'S LONG-TERM FUTURE

September 26, 1995

You know the history of Lake Merritt. Now discover her future.

Joel Harris slipped on his weight belt and eased into the water. As his body adjusted to the 58-degree temperature, he put on his mask and dropped below the surface just past the "Divers Only" sign off Lover's Point across from the International Wildlife Refuge.

He swam slowly across the widgeon grass-covered bottom as a steelhead salmon darted by in pursuit of a topsmelt. Wow! He thought; the underwater video at the Natural Resource Center was right on – they really are more colorful out here.

It was late spring in 2100 and the water visibility was 10 feet. Storm drain pollution had recently ceased to pollute the lake, the tainted sediments had been removed and tidal flushing had been improved in the estuary channel inlet. He swam out to one of the artificial reefs, noting blue mussels, orange sponges and green anemones there. Two webbed feet of a canvasback duck protruded down from the surface and paddled along overhead. Surfacing, he frightened the bird, which fluttered off toward the salt marsh. It was a fine spring day underwater.

*   *   *

Rissaria Jordan was glad she had moved across the Bay from San Francisco to Oakland. The San Andreas quake of 2200 had all but destroyed the Marina neighborhood, and continuing climate change made the city almost unbearable. Oh how she longed for an El Nino year rather than the dry heat that warmed dried out the landscape. She watched as an Orca whale swam into the lake where the 12th Street bridge had been. Hovercraft had made the crumbling structure obsolete, and when the quake destroyed it, planners decided to remove it.

At the new redwood grove by the sea otter release center, she downloaded disks of the last 24 hours of water quality data. The results were good, but with concerning trends. Oh well, with 17 million people in the area, what could one expect?

*   *   *

The grizzly bear dug deeper in the burrowing owl cavity. But rather than a tasty morsel on the hill overlooking the lake, he uncovered only more plastic in the rubble. The year was 4000, but no one was counting. There was no one there to count.

Out on the water 2,000 geese circled and landed in noisy profusion: The latest wave of migrants was flying in from a land once known as Canada. They feasted along the wetlands that now almost covered the open water where two centuries before children had learned to sail.

Darkness fell. A total darkness unbroken by light from the shore. Only in the sky above were there pinpoints of light and a pale moon, curiously marred by red blotches.

The lake was gone; marshlands and mudflats had returned while overhead, the planets and satellites continue their ancient, slow dance. The circle was unbroken.

Note: this essay has been modified slightly from the original to reflect recent events.

59. CONSIDERING THE LAKE'S MOST BASIC ELEMENT

October 24, 1995

When all is said and done, the lake is just water. Call it the jewel of Oakland, a unique urban estuary, our city's most valuable natural resource, the nation's oldest waterfowl refuge or whatever, it's made of water. Just water? Don't let the "just" fool you. Water is pretty remarkable stuff. Consider the following:

Water: It covers three quarters of our planet earth. Consisting of only three atoms (two of hydrogen and one of oxygen), it makes up more than 90 percent of your body and also that of many other living things. Yes, that's right; dry you out completely and less than 10 percent of your weight would remain. Water: Life evolved in it, and mostly still lives in, or very near to it. People who live away from it must bring it to them, or perish. Life cannot live without it.

Consider its properties. In a relatively small temperature range, it transforms from ice to transparent vapor (or fog). The fact that it sucks up heat like a sponge when changing forms makes it an excellent natural air conditioner, which keeps Oakland cool in summer and green in winter. The fact that it bends light makes rainbows; and makes objects underwater look 25 percent bigger (which is no doubt partly responsible for many fish tales). And if that weren't enough, it floats our boats, washes our backs, and mixes well with alcohol! All in all, we're pretty lucky to have 1200 acre feet of it in downtown Oakland.

In addition, it adopts an infinite variety of forms, flavors, temperatures, colors, shapes, and meanings. In clouds, in sunsets, in Jello, and in beer, it enhances our lives. Soothing in the bath, buoyant in the pool, clear if clean, and green if too effused with life, it sparkles in light and keeps our engines (internal combustion and biological) cool. It even reflects our tall buildings, and our souls.

Cooking our food, cleansing our kidneys, washing away our wastes and returning clean again to water our violets, it is the ultimate in recycling. You can't destroy it, but to make it go away, just provide a lower level. Pretty nice stuff. Easy to get along with. Usually predictable, too, if you take time to understand it; flood-control computer models and all that. But then again it makes the weather; got to keep a little mystery about it.

In Lake Merritt, water adopts a salty form, a condition more dedicated to supporting other types of life than human. Uncounted creatures depend upon it. If you were to count the living forms in a hundred square feet of downtown Oakland and a hundred square feet of Lake Merritt's shallow shoreline, the number within the water environment would be hundreds of times greater (most of them unseen). That's quite a contrast. A few humans, lots of grass with a bird or tree or two on one side; and algae, crabs, shrimp, a dozen types of fish, mussels, barnacles, a mermaid, sponges, worms, clams, ducks, geese, widgeon grass, bryozoans, isopods, anemones, and a transient *Homo sapiens* or two just a few yards away. So, step off the edge and enter the realm of life; hatched, fed, nurtured, and protected by the water in Lake Merritt.

What is the net result of all this for Oakland and the Bay Area? For some, it's real estate value. For other, recreation, a pretty view, wildlife, a place to go and stimulus to walk or run. This summer the benefits of Lake Merritt's water may be enhanced by "the Great Race Across the Lake," classes at the Sailboat House, Rotary science Center and Junior Center for Art and Science, and perhaps by dredging the storm drain sediments.

Now you know, Lake Merritt is made up of water, and that is (at least in part) why it is so remarkable.

60. THE BUSINESS SIDE OF NTURAL RESOURCES

December 5, 1995

I never did understand economics, never even had a course in it despite too many years of college. But at seminars and symposia, bars, and around campfires, one can pick up a basic education about the economics of natural resources. Volumes have been written about the topic, but this may be one of the first discourses on the profit, loss, value, and net worth aspects of Lake Merritt.

The lake is of course, a priceless resource. Re-creation of the parkland, the lake bed, islands, shoreline, control structures, infrastructures, superstructures, and associated natural history would exceed our 1995 financial capabilities several fold. Cripes, we can't even afford to maintain it now.

In reality (as some see reality) natural resources don't need maintenance; they maintain themselves. Lakes, oceans, mud flats and such things as Canada geese have been here for ages without maintenance, and always will be. It is the man-made changes that need maintenance, such as the bulkheads along the shore, the artificially deep water that needs dredging, and rangers to protect the geese and ducks from becoming dinner. It is the acts of man (and woman) that result in resource degradation and the need for restoration.

On a more practical level, natural resources are attractions, and can be used to generate income. A restaurant along the water with a bay view will almost always prosper. It has an economic edge over one surrounded by concrete. People will pay to experience what the resource has to offer, be it tranquility, an unusual experience or beauty.

It is also true that many natural resources are owned by public agencies. As such, their care and nurturing are often compromised by budgetary constraints, costs that exceed revenue, and diminishing compensation for the man-made changes that misdirect natural processes.

I once knew an administrator in the National Park Service who told me that during Democratic administrations, park acreage grew as more land was purchased, but when Republicans controlled the budget, no acquisitions were made and maintenance expenditures increased. In the past 20 years he seems to have been right. But today the trend seems to be: Cut the losses and, based on profit and loss alone, eliminate the natural resource, as if government existed to make a profit.

The sad part is that cuts in resource management budgets often lead (in the long term and considering related expenditures) to higher costs and a reduced standard of living for those who can't afford to avoid the ill effects of pollution, blight, and scarcity. Given today's trends the question for Lake Merritt is, can it generate enough income to cope with the maintenance requirements of our actions? Is it considered important enough to pay for lake programs? Is the value of the wildlife refuge considered high enough to support wildlife habitat and use it as a teaching resource?

Several years ago, there was a restaurant between the Rotary Science Center and Sailboat House. Replaced by the Junior Center for Art and Science, it was an example of income generation based on the attraction of the resource. The Junior Center is at an appropriate location for its programs, and should not be displaced. It is self-supporting, and provides a valuable program to make up for what the city cannot afford to do. But given the absence of available funding for needed Lake Merrit restoration, maintenance, and enhancement, is there a way to generate income using the economic advantages of the lake?

Many of the boating programs do that, generating considerable income in fees. But for park maintenance, part-time staff, landscaping etc., an even greater competition for general funds controls the outcome. The squeaky wheel gets the grease, and if we want more funds for Lake Merritt and the park that encompasses it, we must squeak loudly.

If there was a place to site another restaurant without disrupting natural values or existing use patterns, its profits could conceivably be dedicated to the lake and Lakeside Park. Such a concept is not without precedent. In 1995, increased concessions services at Angel Island will offset costs.

Other cost increases at parks will further restrict them to the wealthier among us, a form of economic discrimination, something to be avoided at Lake Merritt. But a restaurant could capitalize on Lake Merritt's beauty and generate revenue for the resource. A public/private partnership would be needed to bear the capital costs and assume the risks, but I strongly suspect that if run right, it would generate a profit.

Like it or not, economics are a reality. We created the need for maintenance and restoration of Lake Merritt. Now can we afford to take care of our own nest?

Note: Since this essay was written, the Lake Chalet restaurant has been established at the lake.

61. APPRECIATION OF WATER IS A RELIGION ALL ITS OWN

December 22, 1995

It was the lower of the two daily low tides: So low was the water that the kayak barely floated near the mud "beach" along 12th Street. The children in front of the boat were complaining, as were the ducks disturbed by our presence. "Why are we here?" he whined. "Why do we come to look at all this stuff anyway?" echoed his sister. "We've seen this lake and these birds a hundred times."

I thought about that. Why do we come back to the water? Is it on the way home, or something required of us? No, but something draws us. When our time is not demanded by money, clocks, or other people, we often choose to visit the lake, to be on the water, to float with the geese and chase the fishes. Time seems to pass by as quickly as the clouds on those days, thoughts filled by the slow movement of the tides and visions on the horizon. Time to observe; time to reflect.

Perhaps it is the lack of pressure inherent in being in such a place. A place with no telephones, a place with no traffic to consume our mind. It is a natural place, a resource created more by nature than by man. Nature moves slower than us, much slower. Not that it is less complicated. No, the complexity is there, but one must work to understand it. It doesn't require your time, but observe long enough, and it will come.

It may have been the wind or a quirky current, but for some reason, the waters parted! There, in the exposed mud, were reflections of the sky. As the boat drifted, the images seemed to shift, like figures in the clouds above. There appeared a cross, a star of David, a peace sign (or was it a giant duck footprint? – they do look alike), and then a smiling bearded face. What was the lake trying to tell us?

I thought about the images several days later, and wondered again at why people go places like the lake, the ocean, mountains, or forest. Perhaps it is because there our senses are open and unencumbered. Thoughts there are free to flow. The subconscious can emerge, answers can come to questions we have pondered, and those not yet asked. But beyond that, beyond our internal thoughts set free by the power of natural resources, I go to the lake because I believe in it. I believe in the laws that control it, what it is, and in its message. Natural resources are teachers. Teachers about our world.

They represent a way of life, a system of beliefs, and to some, a religion. Terry Edwards of the long-gone bluegrass group Cullowhee once sang, "You get a lot more religion a fishin' than you do sittin' in a pew." For many of us, that's true.

Lake Merritt, like many other places with water, sky and life, is a natural resource for the mind. A philosophy and a nourishment to our soul. We are fortunate to have it in among the midst of concrete and steel that is downtown.

So the next time you're out there by the water, pause, listen, and observe. Even if the waters don't part, you can learn a little about the natural world. Your world too, you're a part of it. Part of it's ebbs and flows. And if you believe in the natural laws, maybe your God is out there, waiting to be seen when the waters to part.

62. LAKE'S HISTORY AN ENDLESS CYCLE OF RENEWAL

February 9, 1996

The following is based on an essay entitled "Odyssey" by Aldo Leopold, as published in "A Sand County Almanac", a beautiful, inspiring, and ageless account of the natural world.

X was carried into the lake during a winter storm one January day several thousand years ago. Having been taken from a rock deep in the hills overlooking the bay, it passed into a root, up with the sap, and became part of a seed. The seed floated to the ground one fine autumn day, and was eaten by a squirrel. Passed out to the soil, X had remained there for centuries, but a blink in geologic time.

Gradually moving downhill, X entered a streambed and in a flash was transported to a new world deep in the sediments of Lake Merritt. Entombed there beneath the dark waters, X was eventually washed into a marsh, and there became part of the seemingly endless cycles of growth, death, decay, and renewal. X was part of the cordgrass, of the shell of a snail, a shorebird's bone, and then went back to the mud when a falcon delivered the fatal blow and left part of the bird's tiny body on the shore.

During its era in the lake X was recycled many times and took part in many lives. But always would come death and decay. The bacteria, ever seeking organic molecules to feed upon, would sever the bonds. Released again, X became mineral, but was invariably ingested and the cycle would start again. X assumed many forms, but never changed; indeed was incapable of changing. Combined with others through the attraction of electrons and elemental forces, the bonds were continuously formed and broken. X flew as a feather, swam as a fin, and gave structure to salt grass, all the while residing in and being a part of the physical and living components of Lake Merritt.

Unlike atoms of hydrogen and oxygen which make up water, X was less likely to travel world-wide distances. Those like X that did find their way through the migration of a whale, the flight of a tern or the journey of a ship to the eastern United States found the numbers of their own kind to be far fewer in the uplands. In the sea they existed in a constant, seldom-changing level, but on eastern land the soil and waters were often acid, and were made more so by the far-drifting clouds of sulfur and smoke. In these environments, X made the waters sweeter and the land more fertile. In Lake Merritt, however, X was busy.

The centuries passed, and a new form of life came upon the scene. Powerful, impatient, and single minded, they scooped X out with the bottom mud. Using the energy of harnessed fossil fuel, X was carried out of the lake 20 miles to the west and dumped in a bay near a large bridge. Carried then by the tides on a particle of sediment, X entered the sea, joining its ancient ancestors brought here in eons past. But who knows, fish swim upstream. And perhaps one day X will reenter our lake. Only the mermaid will know.

63. DO YOU FIT THE PROFILE OF A STORM DRAIN POLLUTER?

February 23, 1996

I saw one the other day: A storm drain polluter. He was clothed in bacterial slime and smelled of hydrogen sulfide. His teeth were filed down into long, sharp points, and his hair was oily black and infested with brake lining asbestos. And that wasn't the worst part. His pores were leaking heavy metals like cadmium, mercury, and lead. Pesticides glowed in his wet footsteps and every five minutes he would pull out a chocolate wrapper from his pockets and toss it away. This was no ordinary dude!

So I asked him, "Why do you pollute the storm drain? Don't you realize it drains to Lake Merritt?

"I do? It does?" he said.

As I dared to draw closer, I couldn't help but notice that he was exhaling pure methane. Smudges of fertilizers discolored his pockets and a bubbly film of restaurant grease oozed from his nose.

"I didn't know I polluted the lake," he said. "No one ever told me where the storm drains go."

"It's a really big secret," I replied, "but now that the Cold War is over, the truth can come out. Storm drains don't go to treatment plants."

"Gee, I never knew that," he said. "But does it really matter? Why should I care?"

" Listen," I said. "There's only one thing in this world that really matters ... and that's people who care. If you don't care ... why should anyone care about you?"

And as he walked away, I wondered ... how many people out there are like that? We can all learn not to pollute the storm drain. So be careful. Now that you know what a storm drain polluter looks like ... don't be one!

Storm Drain Legacy

(Adapted from: "The Sky Above, The Mud Below" by Tom Russell)

Two fish swam in from the bay; it was a cold, dark and rainy day

The water above, and the mud below

They passed the entrance channel of shell; and entered the lake as darkness fell

The water above, and the mud below

They came from places in the distant sea; to Lake Merritt where their end would be

To spawn, to recreate was their goal; upon some upstream, gravelly shoal

The water above, and the mud below

Gravel deep and clean they sought; but this life's journey was for naught

Only a dark tunnel and oily scum they found; where once was a stream, now barren ground

The water above, and the mud below

Their time had passed, their lives were spent; what man had wrought would not relent

What once was life was now decay; on the bottom amidst debris they lay

The water above, and the mud below.

64. CAN STRIPED BASS MAKE A COMEBACK TO LAKE?

March 8, 1996

No, this is not about a stripper; it's about a fish ... a fish called the striped bass. A large and powerful predator, silver and black, fast, and it doesn't even need a coliseum like some other silver and black residents of Oakland. Attaining a maximum length of 4 feet and growing up to 90 pounds in California waters, the striper is a challenging sport fish, but recently has all but vanished from San Francisco Bay.

What do striped bass have to do with Lake Merritt? Well, in 1935 they were so plentiful after a high tide that they were taken with pitchforks. In 1930 over three tons of fish (mostly stripers) were found dead in the lake, apparently due to deficient oxygen. Those numbers are hard to believe now, since populations of these popular fish have dwindled to all-time lows. But they still exist here, as proven by their occurrence in recent gill net surveys of the lake's fish populations. Some fishermen also know this, occasionally catching one near the inlet/outlet channel where they feed on topsmelt.

Don't blame Lake Merritt for the decline of the striper. Numbers of this once-abundant fish have dwindled throughout the bay/delta ecosystem. The recent culprit? Freshwater diversions to agriculture. The striped bass is hatched in fresh water, migrates downstream to the sea where it grows to maturity and then returns to its ancestral home to spawn. Unlike most salmon it does not die after spawning, but continues to move between the ocean and fresh water, growing larger with each season. The young fish need a safe, freshwater habitat to grow and replenish the population.

But so much water has been kept from the delta in the past 25 years that the zone of salinity appropriate for the young of these bass has moved upstream from bay to narrow river channels. In short, their breeding habitat has been devastated. In addition, many of the young fish that do make it are sucked into the giant water pumps to be chopped into pieces, or carried by irrigation diversions to dead-end channels where they become fertilizer for sugar beets or rice. Pollutants in the delta system may also have contributed to the decline.

No one alive remembers the time when there were no striped bass on the West Coast: No striped bass; none; zero; nada. Prior to the 20th century, striped bass in the United States were found only on the East Coast. Then, in 1879 and again in 1882, a total of 432 stripers were transported, by train, from New Jersey to San Francisco Bay. The results were astonishing. Without natural predators, parasites or diseases that kept their numbers in check on the East Coast, and with ample breeding grounds in the delta as well as plentiful forage fish, the tiny population thrived, multiplied, and multiplied again. By 1899 (after only 20 years) they had spread from Canada to Mexico. By 1902 the Pacific Coast catch was well over a million pounds.

Then the crash came. As fewer and fewer fish were caught, the state Department of Fish and Game began an annual "striped bass index" to measure their abundance. In 1965 the index stood at 120. By 1990 it had dropped to 4.3 (a decline of 96 percent) and remains low today. Sport fishermen mourn the loss of this outstanding fish, which is as good on the table as on the end of a line. Unless the trends are reversed, fishing for striped bass in the San Francisco Bay system may soon cease to exist.

Can the striped bass return in former numbers to Lake Merritt? Consider this: Each year sections of the California Aqueduct are drained for cleaning. When the water is removed, thousands of fish, including stripers of all sizes, are free for the taking. All that is needed is transportation to the lake, a plan to ensure their care and an appropriate fishing program to qualify for the permit.

The Lake Merritt Institute has submitted grant applications to establish such a program. Included may be a lending library of fishing tackle available free to certified Lake Merritt Anglers. Certification will be granted by attending a class to learn about water quality, safe fishing techniques and environmental stewardship.

We may also establish a striper hatchery to grow and release our own young fish into the lake. If we are successful, we will need volunteer mentors to assist with fishing events and to maintain tackle. Anyone interested in assisting should contact Dr. Richard Bailey at the Lake Merritt Institute (238-2290).

So next summer, if you see a happy kid carrying home a 2 foot-long silver and black fish, think about Lake Merritt, and about how natural resources can enhance human resources, and both can benefit.

Note: The striped bass program never materialized, but a state "Fishing in the City" program did sponsor stocking of rainbow trout, and a few fishing events (see essay # 32). During the 2022 fish kill, dozens of large striped bass died in Lake Merritt. It is presumed that they have since repopulated the lake and are still out there.

65. MAKING AN INVESTMENT IN YOUR COMMUNITY AND ITS RESOURCES

April 19, 1996

This article, the first in a series, is provided by Dr. Richard Bailey of the Lake Merritt Institute and Keith Logan of American Express Financial Advisors Inc. The Institute has teamed with American Express Financial Advisors to establish a Planned Giving Program to benefit Lake Merritt. These articles, and free seminars, are offered as a part of this program.

You probably already know something about the Lake Merritt Institute, about the aeration fountain it installed to improve oxygen conditions, the marine science summer camp called "Eco Aqua," and its plans to restore wetlands and provide an urban fishing program. You may even—we hope—have joined this nonprofit organization.

But you may not know that the Lake has problems that government alone cannot solve, such as urban runoff pollution, the decaying bulkhead walls, and aging public facilities. And, you may not realize the untapped potential of this unique, downtown natural resource.

This article, along with others to follow in The Montclarion, will explain how you can make a "community choice" to redirect tax dollars—capital-gains tax dollars—to your community (and simultaneously to your family) while legally reducing some other taxes and receiving a lifetime income. American Express is conducting this program without cost to the Institute, to participants in the seminars, or those who elect to receive free personal consultations with a financial advisor.

Financial planning tools: In these articles and in seminars to be held this year, you'll learn how people are now beginning to use powerful new financial planning tools—created by Congress and sanctioned by the IRS—to keep more of their wealth. And you'll also learn about your "forgotten wealth," social capital, and how you can reclaim and reinvest it in your neighborhood, town or city as your parents and grandparents once did.

If you could legally put more of your tax dollars to work in your own community, rather than send them to other communities, would you? If you could legally give more of your tax dollars to a specific project in your town, rather than seeing them go to unknown programs elsewhere, would you? If you could direct how and where more of your tax dollars would be used, rather than giving up control of them, would you?

Most people answer "Yes" to all three questions. This is not surprising. It is easy to look around Lake Merritt and see trash that should not be there … piers that need fixing … wildlife habitats that need restoration … sediment that needs dredging …children that need education and fishing.

For example: Mr. and Mrs. Retiree have (fill in the blank with): Assets on which they owe 28-36 percent in capital-gains taxes, or: A house to sell in which taxes would eat up most of their profit, or: Too much money in an appreciated, single stock but which would cost them capital-gains taxes if they diversified it, or: A will but no way to avoid estate taxes. They resent the undeniable fact that if they do nothing, their tax money will be taken away and used to fund who knows what government program.

And they would also like to help kids learn to fish at lake Merritt, where they learned to fish, and to ensure that the Lake will be maintained for future generations. Through the information presented by the Institute and American Express, they will learn about options that will allow them to use the savings in capital-gains taxes to both boost their own income, and help save Lake Merritt.

Reduce taxes, benefit the Lake: But what do charitable gifts you give to local community organizations have to do with taxes? Everything. Because, as previously suggested, charitable gifts offer a legal alternative choice to paying one kind of tax: capital-gains tax.

What's more, if charitable gifts are used wisely as part of your overall financial plan, they can also bring you other benefits as well, including a lifetime income and reduction or elimination of capital-gains taxes and perhaps gift and estate taxes as well. They represent a choice that you can actually make. It's a choice, surprisingly, that few people even know they have.

Next: Our next article in this series will look at the work of the Lake Merritt Institute—and how it has served, and can continue to serve the people, waterfowl, aquatic life, and landscapes of this great urban natural resource. But if you have questions now, call the Institute at 238-2290.

66. RELATION BETWEEN LAND AND PEOPLE

May 3, 1996

This is the second article in a series provided by Dr. Richard Bailey of the Lake Merritt Institute and Mr. Keith Logan of American Express Financial Advisors, Inc. The first article provided an introduction to the Planned Giving Program being established by the Institute and American Express. This article provides more information about Lake Merritt and how you can team up with the Institute and American Express to restore, maintain and enhance this unique, natural, and human resource.

There is, I believe, a relationship between the land and its people. Unseen, perhaps, and unspoken, but it is there. The land affects us in many ways, influences our daily lives, our careers and perhaps even our personalities. You can see it in the difference between a Kansas wheat farmer and a Los Angeles banker. You can hear it in the voice of a New England fisherman or wonder about it when reading of those who live in the desert, on the plains, in northern woodlands or in remote rain forests. Some of us experience our relationship with the land most strongly while visiting isolated mountain areas or while boating on the water.

For the land affects the weather, the climate, the numbers of people who live around us, the daily visual menu that we see and what we eat. It determines what clothes we put on in the morning and, by having influenced the harbors, transportation routes, and therefore the centers of commerce, determines to some extent where we live.

In Oakland, Lake Merritt is part of our land. As public land, it belongs to all of us. It offers opportunities such as jogging, boating, bird watching, and real estate development. It moderates our climate, cooling the land in the summer and warming it in the winter. It provides an open vista to stretch our mind and a patch of green to soothe our soul. But because it belongs to all of us, it is subject to the common tragedy that none of us are forced to take care of it. As a shared resource, we expect the "government" to take care of it.

Unfortunately, the government can't do it alone. No surprise there. And so the land, our Lake, and its central park, suffer. But it is not just the decrepit docks, the dead dogs that remain in the Lake for days, or the medical waste illegally dumped in the storm drain that is the problem. If the real meaning of Lake Merritt is the relationship between the Lake and the people who live around it, then we all suffer.

There is, I believe, a relationship between living in a trashy, unkempt environment and the kid who says, "why should I; no one else does?" There is a relationship between the odors of un-dredged sediment and pervading feeling that the Lake environment is "toxic" regardless of how safe it is. There is a relationship between an environment that is not cared for and people who don't care.

So how does Lake Merritt affect you? Is it enough to move the tax base away to a newer area whose infrastructure has not yet worn out? Or to ignore the place where some of us grew up? If the older, downtown areas succumb to blight, how long will it be before it spreads to the suburbs?

The Lake Merritt Institute is trying to strengthen the relationship between this estuarine resource, its park, and its people. If people work together to improve this area, are they not both better for the experience? If they can feel pride toward the land, toward the Lake, does this not help them feel proud of themselves?

So, this is why we are establishing a planned giving program dedicated to Lake Merritt.

The problem is big, and so is the solution. If the Institute can (by reducing your capital-gains taxes) raise enough money to establish mechanisms that will continue to improve the Lake; if we can continue to keep the lake keeper position to educate, to remind the city and county of their duty; and to organize, then we will have helped not just the environment, but also the people who depend upon it.

If you are interested in reducing the taxes that will be levied on your estate, your capital-gains, and in some cases your income, AND you would like to enhance Lake Merritt's relationship between the environment and people, consider attending our program.

Planned giving is a means of providing funding to the Lake Merritt Institute which benefits the donors as much as the city.

In the next article this spring, we will discuss techniques to reduce taxes and increase your income while helping our Lake.

Call 238-2290 to receive your free invitation to the "Tax Reduction Seminar" on May 9, 10:30 a.m. to noon at the Bellevue Club, 525 Bellevue Ave. Speakers will include Mr. Michael Tillis, CFP, a senior financial planner with American Express Financial Advisors who lives in Montclair. Available space is filling up and reservations are required, so call now. Who knows, that old representative of the Pearly Gates Committee, Sam Merritt himself, may also attend.

67. USING SOCIAL CAPITAL AS A FINANCIAL PLANNING TOOL

May 7, 1996

This is the third article in a series provided by Dr. Richard Bailey of the Lake Merritt Institute and Mr. Keith Logan of American Express Financial Advisors, Inc. The first article provided an introduction to the Planned Giving Program being established by the Institute and American Express. The second article discussed the real meaning of Lake Merritt, and this article provides a case history of how a Charitable Remainder Trust can benefit everyone.

Social capital is that part of your wealth that goes to serve others through either taxes or charitable gifts. A social capital planning tool is one that lets you preserve and direct these funds or assets for the benefit of both you, and the charity of your choice. In one sense it is no different from other financial planning tools that you may already be familiar with, such as insurance policies, wills, retirement savings plans and investment programs. These tools are all intended to help you make the best and most rewarding use of your wealth. A social capital tool is focused on that portion of your wealth that will, unless you make a choice, be taken for taxes to fund government programs.

How is this accomplished? By helping you direct your social capital where it will do the most good for the most people. This means not only the people served your community's charities, but also yourself, your spouse, and your heirs as well. One of the most powerful tools for achieving this is being used by more and more people like you across America. It's called a charitable remainder trust, or CRT for short.

The CRT was created by an act of Congress in 1979 as a way for citizens to make gifts to charity and at the same time build and pass on their estates. CRT's are used by thousands of people today to accumulate wealth, support charitable causes, and build a retirement income. CRT's are used by people in all walks of life and all income levels. In fact, all it takes to benefit from a CRT is a desire to help your community and an appreciated asset like stocks, real estate, mutual funds, or even valuables such as art, jewelry, etc.

Here's an example of how a CRT might work for a couple with some appreciated stock who want to save for retirement. Our couple, the Greens, are both 67, both active in their community, and are preparing for retirement. They own $1 million in stock they bought many years ago for a fraction of its current value. The stock produces very little income. The Greens want to sell the stock and reinvest the proceeds in higher-yielding investments, maybe a mutual fund. What stops them from selling the stock however, is the capital gain they would have on the sale, which would be subject to a hefty capital-gains tax of some $250,000. That means that they would only end up with about 75 percent of the value of their stock to reinvest.

Finding a better way

The Greens are good citizens and they pay their income tax dutifully, but they can't see "donating" one -fourth of their wealth to the IRS if there is a better way. There is a better way, and it's a CRT. All they do is establish a CRT designed to pay them 8 percent of its assets per year. Then they name themselves income beneficiaries and trustees of the trust, and name the Lake Merritt Institute as the charitable beneficiary.

Next, they give their stock to the CRT. Since the CRT is tax exempt, it pays no capital gain tax on the gift. What's more, the Greens get to take a nice charitable deduction on their income tax return. The Greens, (acting as trustees of the trust) sell the stock, and use the proceeds to buy income-producing investments. Thanks to those investments, the trust assets grow. From these assets, the trust pays the Greens their 8 percent ($40,000 a year) for life. The Greens use some of this income to buy life insurance in the amount of $250,000, payable to their children. The rest of the income they use for living, traveling, making some purchases, and doing all the other enjoyable things they've waited so long to do.

Years later, when the Greens die, the balance of the trust assets go to the Lake Merritt Institute. Based on their life-expectancy and the trust earnings, that amount is expected to be at least $500,000. At the same time, the life insurance death benefit passes to their children free of estate tax. In this way, the Greens have "replaced" a significant portion of their wealth they have to insure the continued protection of Lake Merritt.

As you can see, the Greens used a CRT that literally benefited everyone. First, it helped them preserve all the value of their stock, without losing any capital-gains tax. The CRT also paid them a lifetime income to support and enrich their retirement. As for the Lake Merritt Institute, it received a sizable endowment to help it carry on its work in the community the Greens had served and loved. And finally, the children received a significant inheritance.

This is just one example of how versatile a CRT can serve a variety of personal financial planning and community needs. Indeed, a CRT can be given virtually any appreciable asset.

Note: The long term capital gains tax rates for the 2023 and 2024 tax years are 0%, 15%, or 20% of the profit, depending on the income of the filer.

68. IS THERE A DEVIL IN LAKE MERRITT?

May 31, 1996

A devil in Lake Merritt? Evil beneath the waters, lurking on the park shoreline? A case can be made for it, given the gallons of used motor oil, deliberately dumped detergents, and societal chemicals concentrated by a man-made system of convenience and economics, all flowing into what we have made a refuge for birds, fish, and people. And then there is the crime in the park, and a shortage of staff to run city programs. Sounds like a devil to me.

Why here? Why in such a tranquil setting? The answer may lie in the prevalence of common property. In the 1960's Garrett Hardin, a brilliant teacher, wrote what became a classic essay. It was called "The Tragedy of the Commons" and the message bears repeating every few years or so.

In essence, the tragedy (the devil) is a lack of concern over property that is commonly held by all, but owned by no individual. Without a strong owner to protect it, or with no cultural restraints to guide the masses, commonly held resources are exploited, mis-used or even plundered.

Readily understandable examples are the clean air and water resources which we all own, which we all use, but which are difficult to protect. The history of our society has been to use such resources for our personal gain. Individually, such actions may not be a problem. Collectively, especially with ever-increasing numbers, the resource warps, collapses or (as in the case of endangered species) even disappears. That is the tragedy of the commons; the tragedy of collective overuse.

Lake Merritt, a 160 acre estuarine lagoon, which receives the combined runoff of almost 4,000 acres, is a prime example of the devil at work. Thousands of small transgressions combined into a highly visible space serves to remind us that common property needs a stronger voice.

One of the answers is technology. Pipes that go to treatment plants and devices to compensate for pollution (such as our aeration fountain) are examples. Another solution would be a reduced population, but that is not too likely in the short term. A third solution depends on neither technology nor population reduction in that it exists outside the equation:

> *Standard of living equals natural resources times technology divided by population.*

This solution is education, and beyond that, caring. A treasured resource is not exploited, seldom overused, and not degraded. Although this is a difficult message to understand for those with little to lose, it can work if a sense of "that's mine" can be established.

To the extent that we all believe Lake Merritt is mine, our resource will be restored, maintained, and enhanced. To the extent that it is considered belonging to an ill-defined agency or nobody, it will suffer. The commons is ours, but we must act as if it belonged to each of us to protect it.

 The devil is out there: It is up to us as individuals to keep it away.

69. HABITAT: WE ALL NEED IT AND NEED TO PRESERVE IT

September 13, 1996

ROARRRR...! The Raiders of the Last Park were at it again – destroying the habitat. This time they were wiping out another wetland; draining, filling, and paving it over. Ignorance bulldozed the wet soil; Self-Interest dumped the fill; Greed calculated the profits; and Apathy stood by and watched.

"No," cried the mermaid. "The critters need that habitat – for food, for shelter, for breeding areas. How can life live without these things? We'll all be impoverished, homeless, and miserable.

"Wake up, Miska," said Sally Stickleback. "You're dreaming again."

Miska opened her eyes.

"But people don't understand," the mermaid said. "They don't understand about habitat: What good is saving a seal or a baby sea lion without saving it's habitat?"

"It's no good," said the fish. "Now go back to sleep."

She did, and the dreams came again. But this time there were different: The critters were destroying the people habitat! It began slowly. First, they took away all the pizza restaurants (critters like pizza too). But then the critters became more ambitious. They needed food for their growing populations and soon all the restaurants were gone. That hurt. *Homo sapiens* (that's us, you, and me) were forced to live on the basic foods; bare survival. Some of us that could not cook didn't make it; and were found dead in the storm drain where all the stuff no longer wanted ends up.

Next, the critters took away another vital component of human habitat: They closed the streets and roads (which is similar to humans putting up a dam across a river that fish and wildlife use for migration). Eventually the critters destroyed the houses (as we did when we destroyed the forests), the farms (as we did when we polluted the streams and lakes) and even (oh no!) our shopping centers. After they destroyed 90 percent of the cotton crop, there was a shortage of clothes. When the critter predators killed most of our cattle, there were no hamburgers, no cheese, and no milk shakes.

And as the other components of human civilization became overgrown, naturalized, and planted to native species, the populations of people became isolated. The areas they inhabited shrank and soon cousins were breeding with cousins because there was no movement between the groups. Inbreeding began to take its toll as recessive genes built up in the population. We then became endangered, and faced the possibility of human extinction.

But then Miska awoke to her degraded habitat at Lake Merritt with hardly any natural shoreline, no marsh, and pollutants from urban runoff. For it has been man, not the critters, that have ignored the natural laws, and it was she that was endangered, not the human animals. Too bad; the world might be a better place with more mermaids and fewer people.

So what we need then, is more mermaid habitat, more fertile ground in the minds of men and women. And we need more places for things to grow, breed and be wild; not pets or civilized beggars. And we need less concrete, fewer bottom lines, and more listening; listening to the calls of wild geese; listening to the candles burn.

Habitat: We ALL need it.

70. TAKING A LOOK INTO A POSSIBLE FUTURE

Autumn, 1996

The 9.2 magnitude earthquake was sharp and sudden, but its effects were of long duration, and some say may never be reversed. Our lake and its people were split into two, divided by an imaginary line as unreal yet as tangible as a border between two countries. Transportation, commerce, people and eventually even ideas were cut off from each other.

As the years passed, the land on each side of the great divide became quite different. And as the environment changed, so did the people, and as the people changed, they changed the environment even more in an interactive spiral. Feedback loops developed, and the change became even more rapid. To the north was a greener land – cooler from the shade of trees; a land where what the earth and water offered were taken slowly, and no more than could be replenished.

To the south, however, a brown, more barren landscape began to form. Pockets of desolation emerged, dominated by concrete and extremes of heat and cold. It was a land where little life could survive except for transient human forms. Rain, when it fell, disappeared immediately, running off from the hard, impenetrable surface. Organic matter, when it could grow, was quickly snatched up by the unchecked multitudes of people and used for fuel. Faster than it was renewed, clean water and air were consumed, degraded, and spit back into the sorry environment.

As the resources of the south side became deleted and the land less capable of supporting life, more and more people were pushed into poverty. The soil, depleted organic matter and eroded by poor land management, could produce only small harvests. Grazing land could support few cattle and the polluted lake suffered from frequent fishkills as the old, leaking, and unrepaired sewer pipes languished for lack of repair funding (or was it a lack of will?).

Meanwhile, on the northern side of the divide, limits on human activities (indeed on humans themselves) were becoming accepted. Individual freedoms were tolerated, but only in so far as they did not infringe on others, or on the ability of the land and water to follow the centuries old paths dictated by evolution, the time tested measure of ultimate reality. Genes and the information they contained became more and more respected as the pathway of life.

Eventually another type of information (encoded in bits and bytes and able to be electronically replicated and transmitted) emerged. Could this information, if it crossed the great divide, reverse the trends? Could the electromagnetic begin to change how we interact with the biological? And if so, what would the ultimate outcome be? Stay tuned; it may be happening.

Meanwhile, Sam Merritt came back from the dead; and he brought with him the Eleventh Commandment, as written by the great conservationist Walter C. Lowdermilk. And the commandment said:

> "Thou shalt inherit the holy earth as a faithful steward, conserving its resources and productivity from generation to generation. Thou shalt safeguard thy fields from soil erosion, thy living waters from drying up, thy forests from desolation, and protect thy hills from overgrazing by the herds, that thy descendants may have abundance forever. If any shall fail in this stewardship of the land, thy fruitful fields shall become sterile, stony ground or wasting gullies and thy descendants shall decrease and live in poverty or perish from off the face of the earth."

So there you have it. If this commandment is followed, the great divide could not exist, and Lake Merritt and all the land around it would be verdant, productive, and in harmony with its people. Walter Lowdermilk wrote it and Sam said it. Now it is up to us to live it.

71. LAKE AND ITS OFFERINGS AWAIT THOSE WHO TAKE THE TIME

January 3, 1997

Change. Change comes slowly to Lake Merritt, and that is good. We need the reassurance of the ever present geese, the flow of the tides and the enduring features of the landscape. But the moods; the moods change. And we like that. I remember running around the lake 20 years ago, and it was much the same as it is now. The differences are subtle, noticed only by those who know her, by those whose visits are frequent and on a regular basis.

Our lives are typically ruled by a timetable. We are, for the most part, unaffected by the changing seasons or pulses of the sun, moon, and tides. But the lake, she responds to forces that are not controlled by that human metronome, the clock. Tides, for example, are fixed but change by almost an hour daily, so that when we scurry by every weekday at 7 a.m., the tidal stage is slightly different. The lake responds to the pulses of water flowing to and from her. Coupled with the light, changing minute by minute each day, a known yet mysterious pattern of color, movement and life emerges, is born anew like the ever-changing features of a face as time and living make their marks.

It is dawn on a winter's morning, known to the early rowers whose solitude is broken only by the emerging colors of the eastern sky and skittering wing beats of teal as they seek sustenance from the mudflats, uncovered this day and hour by the water. And the lake yields itself to the people and birds who know her moods and patterns. But on this day the weather intervenes, superimposing itself on the celestial mix of tide and light. A hungry wind sweeps against the shoreline, covering its treasures with waves, chilling its inhabitants with water and foam. So go hungry shorebirds; wait until the next cycle and come again to find the nourishment you seek.

Later in the day the wind died. Restless waters were calmed and fog formed from nowhere, dimming the light, silencing the traffic along the shore. As evening approached, they came out of the sky, a few at first and then hundreds of dark forms. An approaching storm had driven them from offshore and the cormorants were seeking refuge and food in downtown Oakland. Unlike the geese or gulls that move onshore as night falls, these birds remain on the water, sparing our docks from their droppings, their warm bodies protected by a thick layer of down feathers. Aligned into the wind and spaced evenly from each other, they remained mostly at the center of the lake until the night passed, then began to dive on the silvery topsmelt that swam below.

On another day there were many life forms; scampering around helter-skelter, arms waving, voices raised and movements furtive. Smoke rose from the grills that crowded the parking lot and noise emanated from amplified speakers. Activity abounded, crowds convened and a patch of green was scarcely to be found. It was Festival of the Lake. But from offshore, with waves lapping gently at the kayak, the figures were ant-like, the sounds muted and motions less intrusive. Distance over water has that effect, and the middle of Lake Merritt is a good place to be when you need a quieter place for reflection.

On a hot day in August an afterglow of the setting sun glittered from the high rise towers, casting sparkles of light across a rippling lake surface. Silently a rowing shell knifed across the water and passed a crew team as the mid-summer darkness grew. And then a strange sight could be seen from the boats. The splashing oars were engulfed in their own light, a bioluminescence created by plankton. It was a cold light, phosphorescent green, gone with the vanishing foam as the tiny cells momentarily flashed and the went dark. Only the rowers seem to have noticed this oceanic phenomenon, carried here from the sea, and flourishing in the lake's nutrient enriched environment.

These are among the many moods of Lake Merritt, open for all to see, embraced by the things wild and free. Constant, changing, predictable, and yielding to the senses, if we are open and receptive. So come; embrace the lake and its offerings. They await.

72. CONTINUITY OF SPECIES A MEASURE OF ENVIRONMENTAL HEALTH

January 24, 1997

Miska (the mermaid) was fascinated. There was something alive in that little glob of jelly. She got up very close to it, inches from her nose, as she watched it. It wriggled! Then, with a burst of energy and a gigantic squirm, it popped out; a miniature stickleback, one of the most common fish in Lake Merritt. Free at last, free at last was the tiny fish. But, as always, with freedom came the requirement to try, came opportunity, came danger.

Other eggs were hatching, too. Dozens of them, deposited in the nest their parents had carefully assembled from bits of plant material. With the slight tidal current they drifted; past the widgeon grass; across the silty bottom; past the outstretched siphons of clams, and the empty coffee cups.

Instinctively, the little jaws snapped and devoured microscopic bits of plankton. Again and again, it dined on the summer soup that is Lake Merritt in July. Growing as it ate, it soon doubled in size, and in a week doubled again. But as it grew, another inevitable phenomenon occurred. Its siblings were disappearing. The one on the left, the one on the right, were gone; victims of the food chain. For although their mother had laid dozens of eggs, only two were needed to carry on the species.

Tale of survival

Unlike most other nature stories written by man, our fish too, is eaten; a meal for hungry sculpin when it ventured too close to the bottom. But its species lived on. Another, luckier, faster of its kind survived to breed, passing along the interaction of stickleback DNA and Lake Merritt environment, to future generations. It is this continuity of the species that is important, not the individual animal. For every life there is (sooner or later, and usually sooner for smaller animals) a death. Under the system of natural laws that we all eventually live by, the individual doesn't matter. Only when brains get overly large does the individual begin to matter to some, but not all, other individuals of its kind. But the big brain experiment is, geologically speaking, rather new. A few more millennia and the insects, or maybe viruses, might rule the earth, not us.

And so we are left with the continuity of species (an inter-breeding mass of life responding to the environment) as perhaps one of the most important measures of environmental health: OUR environmental health. True, species do disappear in healthy environments. But except for mass extinctions such as asteroid strikes, species die out slowly.

When we witness the irrevocable loss of a salmon species because of our manipulation of its environment, it is a signal that we are creating artificial conditions, and artificial conditions tend to have high maintenance requirements (i.e. tax dollars) and tend not to last more than a century or so.

Continue to push an ecosystem and more species are lost, and with them the opportunity to interact with that species, to use it for food, recreation, raw materials or perhaps medicine, and opportunities to understand its true place in the natural world. I think it was William Beebe who said that when a species passes into extinction, another heaven and earth must pass before it can be created again. We don't have that long, and even if we did, wouldn't it be a sad world when the children's book showed what a tiger USED to look like?

Miska, the Lake Merritt mermaid, instinctively knew this. And as she watched over the coming and going of generations, she remained fascinated at the process of life. Join with her in its continuance, not its extinction.

73. TAKING A LOOK AT LITTLE THINGS IN LIFE

April 11, 1997

Copepods. They are the most numerous animals on earth. Except for bacteria, viruses, etc., there are more of them than any other living creature on this planet and several hundred thousand live in Lake Merritt. Nobody knows their exact number, but at times they surely outnumber the people that live in Oakland. Tiny, microscopic, and possessed of two appendages that help them swim, they prey upon prodigious algae in the shadows of skyscrapers.

People like Charles Ford, director of environmental studies at Merritt College, study them, peer at them through microscopes, assign them Latin names and wonder at what they might be doing here.

But do we really know them? Other than capturing a tiny sample of their numbers and watching the captives dart about in a drop of water, we can't communicate. And so we speculate, extrapolate, and imitate. But what if we could enter their world, be one with them and share their connection to all other life forms? What would they be like?

Dawn broke at Lake Merritt and from 90 million miles away, a solar furnace provided the power to rearrange atoms of carbon, hydrogen, and oxygen into simple sugar within a phytoplankton cell offshore of the Boating Center. Photosynthesis was occurring. The keelboats turbulence lifted the cell to the surface as the "Ladies of the Lake" rowed on by. An atom of oxygen was split from carbon dioxide, combined with another of its kind and liberated as pure oxygen gas, soon inhaled by a passing oarsman.

What we call instinct propelled the tiny copepod upward into the zone of light. There, dancing among the drifting, decapod larvae, it feasted on the green cells of life. Within its DNA (as yet unanalyzed by ancestral forms (us)) were all the instructions it needed to survive, propagate, and die, the ultimate measure of all life. The unseen thousands were part of a great chain of life in the lake, one that has existed since shortly after the oceans cooled and plant plankton began to produce our atmosphere. That the copepods were a necessary part of this unintentional relationship was unknown to the microscopic plant cells that color our lake green (or bronze in the winter).

By feeding on the plant cells, the slightly larger crustaceans prevent them from reaching their maximum number where nutrients or some other limiting factor limit further reproduction. Thus, the plant cell population was kept in a constant state of growth, continually renewing the numbers lost to marauding copepods.

Multiply Lake Merritt by all the water in the coastal seas of the world, and you have a vast number of plant cells continually reproducing, producing oxygen, and, more importantly, using up carbon dioxide. The oceans of the world (including Lake Merritt) are a great carbonate sink, one that may just save us from the dreaded greenhouse effect someday.

So the next time you look at the lake and think: "It's dirty," you are probably looking at plankton. It is these millions of cells that keep the lake from looking like a bathtub with 20 feet visibility. And all the while they are feeding the food chain, producing oxygen, using carbon dioxide, and doing their thing as they dance through the water.

74. THE PLANKTON WERE TALKING

September 12, 1997

It had to happen. And where else but at Lake Merritt, a place where those things that live wild in the water are closer to humans than perhaps anywhere else on earth. Charles Ford (Director of Environmental Studies at Merritt College) and Titus Kress (a dock attendant and computer science major at UC Berkeley) were working late one night in the classroom. Charles was peering through the microscope, fussing over the seemingly not-so-random movements of a phytoplankton (plant) sample taken from the lake that night. Most samples are taken during the day, and this night sample was behaving differently.

"The pattern of motion repeats itself," said Charles. "It almost seems like they are trying to communicate with us, like bees do with their dance after they've found a new pollen source."

"Hmmm," mused Titus. "Perhaps we can analyze it." Titus was re-configuring the bank of computers that were networked in the classroom. "What if we route the microscope image into the computer camera, and then to the scanner? We could connect the output to the random pattern program, and from there to the new voice operator that mimics human speech."

Charles was always up for an experiment, even at 1 a.m. "Let's try it," he gushed.

In minutes Titus had hooked up the apparatus. At first the speaker just said: Bozzly, Boozly, Brizangapon. "That sounds like James Joyce" said Titus, as he adjusted the frequency modulator. The next words were astounding, and will certainly put Lake Merritt on the map along with the great discoveries of Atlantis, Booneville, and Lake Woebegone. The plankton were talking.

"You are too big," came the message.

"And you utilize energy inefficiently."

"Wow" said Charles.

"How perceptive," said Titus.

"Why do you not worship the sun" said the tiny plants?

"Well, we did at one time" said Charles, "but we stopped: I'm not sure why, something to do with gasoline I think."

"And why does your kind make all these plastic bags and things that will not decompose into simple elements that life can use?"

"Well, er … it has something to do with money," said Titus, "so some people can have more of it."

"We don't want your money," said the plankton. "We would rather have energy; that's more important."

"Why do you destroy the marshes? Why do you build docks and not maintain them? Why do you pollute the storm drains?"

"Uh" … said Charles.

"Well, some people don't know any better," said Titus.

"But we'll teach them," said Charles.

And so he did; taking the little plankton samples with him to schools around the country. The *Message of the Plankton* was spread far and wide. Soon it will be at your school, in your home, and even on TV. Watch for it: Abide by it.

75. MISCONCEPTIONS ABOUT LAKE MERRITT – GRADE YOURSELF

November 7, 1997

Lake Merritt is probably the most misunderstood body of water in the world. To test YOUR knowledge of the Lake, grade yourself according to the following:

Kindergarten: If you believe the Lake is fresh water, not salty, your knowledge is at the kindergarten level. Don't feel bad: Lots of people think that because it is called a "lake," the water is fresh.

Second Grade: If you know that the Lake is not polluted with sewage, advance to the second grade. Except during heavy rainstorms when the ground is saturated or when sewer lines break, all sewage flows to the EBMUD treatment plant.

Fourth Grade: If you know there are thousands of fish in the Lake, join the fourth grade. Don't believe it? Then stand still and stare into the water along the shoreline sometime.

Sixth Grade: If you know the Lake has been here for over 10,000 years as a tidal lagoon, and was not originally created by people, enter the sixth grade. Sorry Sam Merritt, the Creator beat you to it.

Eighth Grade: If you know that there are thousands of shrimp in the Lake, move up to the eighth grade. Unfortunately, they are only about two inches long; not big enough to eat.

Tenth Grade: If you are aware that 5,000 acres of streets, parking lots, rooftops, and lawns drain into the Lake, congratulations! Move up to the tenth grade.

High School Graduate: If you know that the Lake is safe for body contact (e.g. swimming, wind surfing (which kids do all summer) etc.) you're ready for college! Most people just look at the trash and assume the water is polluted.

College Graduate: If you realize that plankton, not silt, is what limits the clarity of Lake Merritt's water, join the "in group." The "out group" thinks it's mud.

Board of Directors: If you answered most of the questions correctly, and you think the city doesn't spend enough money on the Lake (fixing docks, enhancing wildlife habitat, maintenance, and security, etc.) join the Institute Board of Directors: We need you!

Disappointed at your level? Then join the Lake Merritt Institute and learn more about this downtown sailing Lake / wildlife refuge / scenic treasure etc. Members are "cognoscenti" (a Latin word meaning those who know about the Lake).

For as little as $10 (or more if you really want to help) you can be a member. Just call 238-2290 or email the Institute at:

info@lakemerrittinstitute.org

We'll send bulletins and other information designed to reveal the Lake's secrets, and improve your score.

(Note: Memberships now begin at $15.00; hardly an increase since 1997).

76. MISCONCEPTIONS

December 5, 1997

I don't know what their names were, but someone had probably named them. They were two ducks; white, domestic, and obviously bred by the hand of a man since nature does not allow such white birds to live long in the wild. But men (and women) can be fickle … uncaring and cruel. And so it was that they were abandoned, dropped off in the parking lot and left to survive on their own at Lake Merritt.

As the "Central Park" of Oakland, Lakeside Park and Lake Merritt are often the place where no longer wanted pets are left to fend for themselves. Creatures such as peacocks, albino pigeons, cats, dogs, and Easter chicks grown too large to be cute are all too often taken from their human homes and pushed out the door of a car on the shores of Lake Merritt. What follows is not pretty.

One of the ducks (the likely victim of a car driven too fast) was dead in the parking lot, motionless. The other, obviously its mate, refused to leave the lifeless body. It lay there next to the limp form as if to keep it warm. If frightened away, it always returned. Finally, a park ranger removed the corpse.

Darkness fell, and I returned to the site where the dead bird had been. Sadly, the remaining white duck was still there, nestled a few feet from where its friend had lain. It crouched behind the "Keep Right" sign, head tucked behind a wing. Where else was it to go? It knew nothing of the landscape. Only the site where its companion had died. The life-giving Lake, the noisy sea gulls, the people passing by, were all alien, strange, and threatening.

What happened next was a sad testimony to the cruelty that our society can create in its youthful inhabitants. While this column typically reflects on the joys of the natural world, there are some out there who do not share the values, who are insensitive to the plight of an abandoned animal. Being a biologist, I do not profess to be one who extols the sanctity of a wild animal's life. Evolution cares for the species, not the individual.

But a pet, an animal imprinted on a person and dependent since birth on our care for its survival, is different. It is not a wild, free, and independent life form. It is one who prefers the assurance of a next meal to the call of the wild and the ability to come and go as it will. It is rather (having known no other life) an animal dependent upon its owner for its existence. It is a creature of our making, and often too trusting.

The teenagers in the parking lot did not know this. They picked it up and carried it to their car. Observing, but not having seen a violation and wishing to avoid a confrontation, I called police dispatch. "All agents are busy" said the recording ... For a full five minutes. Finally, I gave up.

Hours later I returned to the parking lot. The duck was gone; nowhere in sight. I checked the bushes: No duck. It was then that I noticed the upside-down cardboard trash box. Instinctively I picked it up, and out came the duck. Call it youth, call it whatever, but they had left the animal trapped in and 18 by 18-inch box. Free at last, free at last, it waddled over to the shoreline. By the next morning, hunger had driven it into the water where it drank the salty water and nibbled at algae. Thankfully, a Rotary Ranger rescued the bird and brought it to the duck pond where fresh water, food, and companionship were available. Fate had taken its mate, but the life force compelled it to survive.

Oh, I did stupid things as a teenager too, but never to a pet. Apparently, some people don't (can't) care. The lesson? The way to make it better? Difficult, if not impossible. An often empty parking lot cannot be permanently patrolled. But if those that use it would be more aware, if the police dispatch number were not so busy, if people would refrain from leaving their animals at the park, perhaps the duck (and you and I) could be spared the specter of a pet left alone, confused, and afraid.

Don't abandon pets at Lake Merritt. Call the Rotary Nature Center at 238-3739. They will help find a home for it. Lake Merritt is for wild animals, free and unwilling to be tamed. Given the inability of some people to care, it's better that way. Let pets be pets, but let wild animals be wild. They prefer it that way.

77. PORTRAIT OF A RAIDER

December 19, 1997

The lake critters were swimming around and talking the other day. "They're at it again," said Miska the Mermaid. "Those cursed *Raiders of the Last Park.*" (You and I know them as Apathy, Greed, Self Interest, and Ignorance) but Miska just calls them the Raiders. "This time that Apathy raider is pretending we don't exist," said our favorite mermaid.

It was true. Apathy had indeed been at work. While his cousins (the deterioration sisters) had been busy breaking down the lake's infrastructure (docks, boats, programs, staff, shoreline, etc.), Apathy had been busy sowing his seeds. And they grew: Grew like cobwebs in the minds of good people. And so when the time came for renewal, and for rebirth, nothing happened. Initiative was stillborn, rainbows faded and opportunities melted into the mist. Apathy smiled and Ignorance grinned because the lake and its meaning to people were being ignored.

"Of course we exist" said Pete the Pipefish. "People just can't see us because we're all covered with water."

"Some people say we aren't important just because we're not endangered or dangerous" said Sally Stickleback.

"Yes, but those endangered ones, like the steelhead trout; they represent us" said Miska. "When the endangered and dangerous species are saved, we are all saved. So they represent us; kind of like a representative or a councilmember or something"

"You mean like a Nadel or a Russo?" said Pete.

"Yeah, kind of like that," said Sally. "But do people, like councilmembers, get endangered or dangerous too?"

"They're only dangerous to us if they ignore us" said Miska, "but that's when they become endangered by the people who really care about us."

"Well, I heard that they do care," said Sally.

"And that they'll help fix up this old lake," said Pete.

"Well, I'm worried about that Apathy raider" said Miska. "He's the one who thinks it is OK to have all these busted docks, artificial wildlife habitat and trash floating around."

"Yeah, they call this a wildlife refuge, but it doesn't even have a marsh" quipped Pete.

"We want a MARSH yelled the baby goslings."

"And fishing docks and fish to catch" said the school kids who were listening in on the conversation (the lake is for people too you know).

"So let's get that Apathy raider" they said in unison. "But how? We can't just ignore him; we've got to do something. Ignoring apathy is apathy; and ignore is 66 percent of ignorance. So let's get involved; write our councilmembers; join the Lake Merritt Institute and call the editorial page editor."

"That'll do it" said Miska, "we'll frazzle that Apathy raider; send him to the storm drain where he came from."

So beware out there any apathetic raiders. You don't want to be sent to the storm drain.

(Note: Nancy Nadel and John Russo were council members who supported Lake Merritt).

-30-

INTERLUDE

A YEAR IN THE LIFE OF LAKE MERRITT

Written by Dr. Richard Bailey: September, 2002
Note: As of 2024, some aspects of this essay are currently outdated.

INTRODUCTION

Just as summer, fall, winter and spring sweep across the land, so do these seasons effect Lake Merritt. As one month changes into the next, the appearance of the Lake changes; one day murky and brown, the next sparkling and clear. Algae, trash, and waterfowl appear as if out of nowhere, and then vanish. Throughout the year, these natural cycles are blended with man-made events, forming a collage that is relatively unique to this lagoon, but also common to other aquatic worlds.

This "panorama of time" unfolds before us every year, although much of it cannot be easily seen. Underwater, a myriad of plants and animals follow natural laws and instincts as they cope with the changes that we have imposed on their life cycles. Sometimes we marvel at their beauty and fecundity; sometimes we complain about the smell. The seasons present both opportunities and challenges.

Why do these things occur, and what can we learn from them? This calendar is an attempt to capture with words some of the natural phenomena that the Lake exhibits to us. It is however, only accurate to the extent that we have observed and understand these events. Many of these themes have been poorly studied at the Lake, and are therefore not well understood. There is much to be learned, such as how much nitrogen cycles through the Lake and its impact on seaweed growth. It is our hope that publishing this calendar will help people better understand how Lake Merritt works, thereby leading to a better understanding, appreciation and management of this multiple-use, natural resource.

FUNDAMENTAL ELEMENTS OF A LAKE CALENDAR

Rainfall/Runoff: More than anything else, Lake Merritt is impacted by rainfall and urban runoff from the 4,670 acre watershed. Water from this area flows downhill and enters the Lake through 60 storm drains, diluting salt water from the Bay and bringing trash, car wash soap and anything else dumped on the pavement into the Lake. The Lake Merritt Institute maintains a rain gauge to help us predict how much trash will be in the Lake after a storm. Recent monthly averages in inches at our gauge have been: January - 6.42; February - 9.77; March 2.28; April - 1.44; May - 1.09; June - 0.07; July - 0.05; August - 0.24; September - 0.34; October - 0.97; November - 3.84; and December - 3.43.

Tidal Flows: Most of the water you see in Lake Merritt came from San Francisco Bay via twice daily tidal flows. Computer modeling by a professional hydrological firm has shown that Lake water has an average residence time of about four days. Actual flows however, are highly variable. For a better understanding of tides, click on the "Tidelines" button at our website.

Unfortunately, tidal flows are muted by the shallow channel connecting our Lake to the Oakland Inner Harbor. Narrow constrictions where the tidal channel crosses 10th and 12th Streets limit flows to and from the Lake. While the Bay experiences a tidal range of 6.4 feet, the range in the Lake is only 1.5 - 2.0 feet. For more details, see the White Paper on Tidal Flows at our website http://www.lakemerrittinstitute.org/.

Flood Control: Water levels at Lake Merritt are controlled by a flood control station using tide gates and pumps operated by Alameda County. The station is designed to handle storms up to those statistically likely to occur once in 25 years. Larger storms, such as a 50 or 100 year event, will cause flooding. Lake Merritt floods when the water exceeds 3.0 feet as shown on the Lake's six tide gauges. When this level is exceeded, there will be water on the shoreline path in a few locations, offices at the Boating Centers may flood, and the parking lot by the boat ramp will be slightly inundated. However, during much of the rainy season, you will see the Lake at an elevation of only 1.0 feet because the Lake is held artificially low for flood control. The two foot difference is flood control capacity over the Lake's 140 acres.

Floods can occur when runoff from rainstorms coincides with an incoming tide. To reduce the chance of this happening, The County Flood Control District operates tide gates and a pumping station along the Estuary Channel. Although the pumps are almost never used and tide gates are normally kept open, incoming tides are restricted if there is a 50% chance of rain in a forecast received twice weekly by the district. Restriction of incoming tides exacerbates the low oxygen problem that often occurs in the winter. Low oxygen occurs in the bottom layer of water, which cannot drain because the outlet is five feet higher than the Lake bottom. *(Note: This problem was largely eliminated when the 12th St. outlet was rebuilt in 2013).* This bottom layer is not flushed when high tides are kept out of the Lake due to flood control.

Plant Growth (plankton, algae, and widgeon grass): Lake Merritt exhibits dramatic changes in appearance as aquatic plants go through their natural cycles. Although unseen except through a microscope, one celled plants called plankton dominate the Lake during most of the year. They are the reason the water typically appears murky, green, brown, and even almost red.

Algae (mostly *Enteromorpha* and *Cladophora*) grows in large quantities during the spring and early summer, but only in the shoreline area where depths are four feet or fewer. Although a very beneficial part of the food chain, it becomes a nuisance when there is too much of it, causing odors and depleting oxygen levels when it decays. Algae is kept in check by removal with the harvester boat, operated by the Oakland Public Works Agency.

Widgeon grass is a rooted plant that grows from tubers across much of the Lake bottom, reaching lengths of 10 feet and requiring removal by the harvester boat. Each year this plant spreads to ever increasing areas of the Lake making it harder to control. For details on its growth patterns, see the discussion under spring and summer below.

Algae growing on widgeon grass creates towers which billow up from the Lake bottom in the spring.

Urban Runoff: Every month the Institute removes between 1,000 and 7,000 pounds of trash from Lake. Merritt. During months when there is less than one inch of rain, the average removed is 1,840 pounds. During months when there is more than one inch, the average removed is 4,475. Obviously, most of the trash is carried in by rain. This trash includes dozens of cigarette lighters (we made them into a sculpture) thousands of plastic bags and wrappers, hundreds of bottles and cans, uncountable pieces of Styrofoam and thousands of cigarette butts. Interestingly, we have also removed dentures, a cell phone, a no littering sign, a safe, a television set, an armchair, a parking meter, unmentionable clothing, a football trophy, a hand carved pumice candle holder, a fire extinguisher, an assault rifle, a clay mask, drugs, numerous car parts, and a magic wand.

Oakland's first storm drain filter was installed at Lake Merritt in September, 2001. This new technology has no moving parts and requires minimal maintenance. It removes many pollutants from urban runoff before they reach the lake.

Water Quality (oxygen, salinity, visibility, and bacteria): Lake Merritt's water quality is constantly changing in response to tidal flows, urban runoff, plant growth, numbers of waterfowl, and management activities such as lake level control and plant harvesting. Based on monthly bacterial monitoring by Alameda County, the Lake is suitable for body contact such as swimming and windsurfing during the dry season. After a heavy rain, the Lake stratifies into an upper, fresh water layer and a lower, salty layer. The United States Environmental Protection Agency has listed Lake Merritt as an impaired body of water due to trash and low oxygen conditions, which occur in the bottom layer. The salinity ranges from fresh water behind barriers at creek outlets to near that of sea water at the Lake center during the summer. Visibility is determined by plankton density, which is determined by nutrient availability and competition with seaweed. Overall, the Lake is a highly enriched tidal lagoon, over-fertilized by urban runoff.

Biological Activity: In 1870 the California legislature passed a law making it illegal to take, kill or destroy any wild animal in Lake Merritt and within 100 rods of the high water mark. Although this law created the nation's first wildlife refuge, these restrictions have since been generally extended to the entire County, thus making the refuge similar to other areas of Oakland. But preservation of natural habitat (even though only in remnants) and continual feeding has created a refuge for waterfowl and many forms of aquatic life in the midst of a high density urban area. The park's wild (and semi-domestic) animals are admired and enjoyed by thousands of people every day.

About 90 species of birds are known to visit or permanently inhabit the refuge, including Canada geese that number over 1,500 during the early summer molting season.   Fish species include small leopard sharks, topsmelt, sticklebacks, gobies, sculpin, surfperch, pipe fish, striped bass, salmonids, bat rays and halibut.

SPRING (March - May)

Summary: Life blooms in the water as warmer temperatures and longer days stimulate breeding by fish, birds, and plants. Plankton flourishes while barnacle and shellfish growth begins. Worms can be seen spiraling underwater in their spawning dance. As rainfall diminishes, trash becomes less visible, and water quality improves. Normal tidal flows become more common as the threat of floods subsides, reducing the chance of odors. Underwater, widgeon grass growth begins in April and becomes noticeable in May. Algae, absent in March, dominates the shallows in May. From high rise buildings the shallow shoreline may appear as green as a lawn. By late spring, goslings and baby mallards delight almost everyone, including seagulls that feed on them.

Rainfall: The average precipitation measured in our gauge at Lake Merritt between 1998 and 2001 dropped from 2.28 inches in March, to 1.44 inches in April, and 1.09 inches in May. Big storms are less common, and rainfall typically occurs on ten, four and three days in these spring months. Creek and storm drain flows are cleaner, with little woody debris and few leaves.

Tidal Flows and Flood Control: As rainfall and the threat of floods both diminish, the County Flood Control District allows the tide gates to remain open during high tides more often. Salt water inflow occurs more frequently, mixing with the bottom waters of the Lake and improving oxygen levels in this layer. This increased flushing removes urban runoff pollutants and stimulates biological growth. At the 7th Street flood control station, all tidal flows must pass through bars that are only 4 inches apart. Every other bar at the bottom is cut to provide 7.5 inch openings as shown here at the right side of the photograph. This is known to limit large bat rays from entering the Lake.

Plant Growth: In May, several types of algae grow vigorously in the shallow waters. Most common are light green filaments of *Cladophora* and *Enteromorpha*, along with the darker green sea lettuce (Ulva). This growth is limited to 20 - 25 feet of the shoreline where the water is only zero to four feet deep. At greater depths, light penetration is not sufficient for growth. By mid-May, algae may cover the entire shoreline area out to deeper water, blanketing the area in bright green where only

murky water existed just a month before. Towers of algae billow up, providing both shelter and food for both fish and invertebrates. Patches of black, velvet like material (probably bacteria) grow on the bottom and break off, floating around and giving the Lake a bad reputation from those who do not understand that this is a natural event.

Prior to dredging, algae dominated in the spring

<u>Urban Runoff</u>: The average amount of trash removed between 1998 and 2001 for both March and April exceeded 3,500 pounds, but by May this figure drops to 1,885 pounds. Since trash removed is a measure of trash in the water, the Lake looks cleaner in late spring, a welcome sight after months of litterbug leavings on display in the shallows. As the season ends trash seen in the water is mostly hand thrown and windblown, not washed in through storm drains.

Storm drains carry litter, animal waste and road film to Lake Merritt. Illegally dumped oil, cement, paint, anti-freeze et cetera also flow (untreated) to the Lake, entering it through sixty storm drain outfalls, which are numbered around the shoreline. If you see illegal dumping of hazardous waste, call 911. For other illegal dumping and littering, call the City Litter Enforcement Officer at 434-5101.

<u>Water Quality</u>: Water quality improves dramatically in the spring. The combination of less urban runoff and increased tidal flows results in fewer man-made chemicals (oil, soap, fertilizer etc.) entering the Lake and a healthier bottom environment. The stratification into top and bottom layers that marked wet winter months occurs less often. Oxygen levels are less of a problem during this time as photosynthesis (which produces oxygen) increases in response to longer day length and warmer temperatures.

Students from the Oakland High School Environmental Academy take weekly water quality samples during the school year. In 2002 the City of Oakland installed two continuously recording water quality monitoring buoys to measure oxygen, temperature and salinity at the surface and bottom. *(Update: These monitoring buoys were temporary, but in 2023, three 24/7 monitors were installed).*

As the season progresses, the water becomes saltier, allowing marine organisms to flourish. Nutrients however, are plentiful, having been deposited in the sediment from leaves and other organic matter washed in all winter. Spring applications of lawn fertilizer at golf courses, cemeteries and homes also end up in the Lake, especially if excessively used and applied before a rain.

Biological Activity: Just as March roars in like a lion and goes out like a lamb, spring sees the diminishing of winter's migratory ducks. At winter's end the embayment by the Nature Center still hosts hundreds (or more) of them. By late May they are gone, leaving the Lake to the year round residents, most of whom are busily breeding. By early April the first goslings of the season have hatched, followed later by mallard ducklings, which often end up as dinner for voracious seagulls. The boat barrier across the Trestle Glen arm is removed as rowers go where rafts of scaup, teal and coots recently slept.

Little is known about when the Lake's various fishes spawn here, but by mid- April the shallows are full of tiny fish fry. On calm nights the surface is alive with ripples as breeding activity increases. Juvenile surf perch have been found in the Lake, and it is likely that topsmelt and sticklebacks also breed at this time.

Those who stroll around the shoreline may see the curious spiraling dance of reddish polychaete worms as they go through their spawning ritual. Other invertebrates (animals without backbones) are also busy flooding the water with eggs which hatch into larvae and swim around. Barnacle and mussel growth is quite rapid in the spring and tens of thousands of half inch long mussels can be seen in the shallow waters. Within only a few months they will be full grown at 3 - 4 inches long.

SUMMER (June - August)

Summary: June is a month of transition as algae disappears and widgeon grass takes over. By July, boating classes have started and the Lake is filled with colorful sailboats, kayaks, and canoes. Wind surfers sail, fall, and climb back up again. Goose numbers increase dramatically as molting birds from elsewhere seek out the sanctuary of the park (and leave large quantities of fecal material on the lawns and sidewalks). Pelicans and terns return, amazing us with their aerial acrobatics as they dive for topsmelt and other small fish. Lake waters become extremely clear, then revert back to their murkiness. Water temperatures rise and clumps of red algae appear, as do crabs and shrimp. Trash removed from the shoreline is minimal but still exceeds 1,000 pounds per month. Spills of paint are sometimes seen entering the Lake from storm drains as home improvement activity and illegal dumping increase. Flood control is not a problem, but the tide gates are still typically closed for two days a week so that Lake elevation can remain high for the harvester boat. By August, the widgeon grass is gone and increased numbers of cormorants can be seen diving on schools of fish.

Summertime means boating at Lake Merritt

Rainfall: Rain is essentially absent during these summer months, averaging less than 0.1 inch in June and July and less than 0.25 inch in August. This is both good and bad as urban runoff is greatly reduced, but trash builds up on the streets, in storm drains and in creeks, waiting to be flushed into the Lake. When an unusual summer storm does occur, it can wash large quantities of trash as well as bacteria from avian feces into the water.

Tidal Flows and Flood Control: Without rain, there is no threat of floods. But the tide gates are still closed for two days during the week so that water levels can be kept high for operation of the harvester boat. This allows it to work closer to the shoreline where cut pieces of widgeon grass and algae accumulate. During these days, the Lake is prohibited from draining, and high tidal flows are kept out. Other exceptions occur when the flood control structure is cleaned of barnacles, mussels, and tube worms by divers, and when Oakland requests continued high water on a weekend for boat races.

Plant Growth: Just as shoreline algae dominates the Lake in late spring, so does widgeon grass dominate in early summer. This grass is not a type of algae, but a rooted plant that produces seeds. It became prominent in the Lake in the 1970's, was mostly removed by dredging in 1985, and has been growing back ever since then. It flourishes during periods of maximum day length and light intensity, and grows up from the bottom to lengths of eight or more feet across parts of the Glen Echo arm and much of the Lake center.

In June & July, un-counted tons of widgeon grass are removed from the Lake.

If uncontrolled by the City's harvester boat, it can severely restrict boating, foul the waters when it rots, and produce odors. Uncounted tons of it are removed as the Public Works Agency works seven days a week during the peak growing season. As the Lake slowly fills with sediment and the grass spreads, control by the harvester becomes more demanding. Eventually, widgeon grass growth will exceed the capacity of the harvester to remove it. In recent summers large quantities of the rotting grass have accumulated along the shoreline. By late July to early August, it finishes its growing cycle and it gone.

Long term control can be achieved by dredging, which removes the roots from which the plant grows. An ideal situation would be to harvest from May, July, and dredge during August and September. This is recommended in the Lake Merritt Master Plan, and would require the city to obtain its own small dredge boat at a cost of about $100,000. Shoreline algae reappears in August, but at much lower quantities than in the spring.

Urban Runoff: Trash in the Lake is at a minimum during the summer, but litterbugs still manage to deposit about 1,000 pounds per month. Some of this comes from vandals who throw City trash containers directly into the Lake. In the summer of 2001, five of the cardboard boxes were pulled from the shallow waters after their accumulated trash had sunk or drifted away.

Unfortunately, with the reduction in trash comes an increase in pollution from oil, soap, paint, cement, plaster, and other home improvement activities. This is most often visible near the outfall of Glen Echo creek, where the channel leading to the Lake sometimes turns white, fish die and plants are killed. In 2001, nine such spills were recorded from Glen Echo creek and an additional 21 spills were recorded from other storm drain outfalls around the Lake

With increased summer activity around the Lake, unusual items also find their way into the water. Among our "Catches of the Day" are: A bowling ball, a bridal veil, a 3.5 foot long striped bass, a clay mask, a metal toilet paper dispenser, a folding chair, a 15 inch dildo, a four inch thick foam mattress and a fire extinguisher. Shopping carts are another favorite of vandals; three of them were removed in the summer of 2001.

Water Quality: Except for bacterial levels, no recent data on water quality exist for the summer, but this information is being gathered in 2002. The absence of this information prevents conclusions from being drawn regarding stratification and oxygen levels. Water quality in Lake Merritt during the summer is adequate for body contact sports, including wind surfing and swimming.

Water clarity however, increases to as much as 7 - 10 feet in June during the peak growing season for widgeon grass. Along the shoreline and across much of the Lake's center the bottom is visible, showing us a myriad of plants, fish, mud, and shells. This clarity is thought to result from greatly reduced plankton (microscopic plant life) growth, which is probably due to a reduction of available nitrogen. Where does the nitrogen go? A simple glance at the widgeon grass gives the answer. But when the grass finishes its growing cycle and dies in July, nitrogen is returned to the system, plankton again flourishes and water clarity decreases. During the summer, the Lake essentially shifts from a system dominated by plankton to a system dominated by rooted plants, and back to plankton domination again. This is why water clarity changes.

Biological Activity: "Gee, there really are fish in the Lake" is often heard during the summer as millions of gobies, sculpins, sticklebacks, topsmelt and even pipefish move into the warm, shallow waters where they can be seen. And there to feed on them are the wading birds; snowy and common egrets by day and black crowned herons by night. In July of 2002, 197 snowy egrets were counted at the Lake, shaking their yellow feet to scare up fish.

Patches of pink - purple bacteria are sometimes seen along the shallow shoreline in areas where widgeon grass and algae are decaying. The bacteria break down plant material, just like composting.

Geese however, now dominate Lake Merritt in the summer. When their molting season begins in late May - early June, numbers of these birds at the Lake increase from several hundred to as many as 1,800 or more. Since each bird defecates about as much as an adult person, many areas of lawn and sidewalk become fouled with fecal material during the summer. Lawns become impossible to use for picnics, and large areas of the shoreline are covered with excrement.

It wasn't always this way: Prior to the mid-'40s, Canada geese appeared only rarely at Lake Merritt. By the mid-90's, their numbers had grown to about 300 - 400 birds. This increase mirrors the national situation, and at numerous golf courses, athletic fields, and other cities with too many geese, their numbers have been reduced by management practices.

At Lake Merritt however, the birds are not managed, and the numbers keep increasing. By summer's end the molting season is over, some two year old birds fly away, and the number of geese at the Lake declines to a level that is less likely to spread diseases such as avian cholera and botulism. These threats however, are very real in the summer.

(Note: Tables, graphs, and photographs from the original "A Year in the Life of Lake Merritt" are not included here, but may be seen at the Lake Merritt Institute website: https://lakemerrittinstitute.org/wp-content/uploads/2018/03/A_Year_In_The_Life.pdf

AUTUMN (September - November)

Summary: The season begins quietly as westerly winds diminish and day length becomes shorter. Storm drain flows are minimal, originating mainly from irrigating lawns and washing cars. Slight algal blooms return after the last of the widgeon grass has decayed away. Spawning is over for most species, but cormorant numbers increase and coots appear.

Autumn is a season of change at Lake Merritt as summer birds fly south, winter migrants arrive and urban runoff begins to cause deteriorating water quality. While Lake visibility is often good in September, it will always drop to 3-4 feet by late fall due to increased blooms of plankton. School resumes and sailboats are seen less frequently on the water, replaced by colorful floating leaves. Someone usually throws a pumpkin in the Lake after Halloween, and the Lake is sometimes a topic of fall political campaigns or bond measures.

By autumn, trash has been building up for several months in storm drains, on streets, sidewalks and elsewhere in the watershed. When the first rainstorm hits, it will be mobilized into "The Big Flush" and flow downstream into Lake Merritt.

Rainfall: The rains begin slowly with a recent average of only 0.34 inches in September. By October precipitation has increased to 0.97 inches, and in November bigger storms hit, dropping an average of 3.84 inches. Because a large percentage of Lake Merritt's watershed is impervious, the water runs off quickly. As fast as the water falls, storm drains and what few creeks remain carry it down to one of the 60 outfalls, and into the Lake.

Millions of dollars are spent on bringing water to the Bay Area and Oakland from as far away as the Sierra mountains. Almost equally large sums are spent to carry water away in storm drains and flood control channels, getting rid of it as soon as possible. Storing rainfall in the watershed for later re-use as irrigation could provide many benefits, including:

- Reduction of imported water and associated costs

- Less cost for flood control and fewer floods

- More natural stream flows and healthier riparian systems

- Diminished negative impacts to water quality in Lake Merritt and beyond.

Such storage could take the form of fences that hold 10,000 gallons of water, underground tanks at individual houses or small wetlands and retention basins. These tools are currently being employed in the Los Angeles basin, but are scarce in the Bay area.

Tidal Flows and Flood Control: Because there is little rain in the first few months of fall, flood control is seldom required. Muted tidal flows enter and leave the Lake twice daily through tunnels at 12th Street, and the shallow, narrow channel leading to the Oakland Inner Harbor. By late autumn however, a 50% chance of rain may cause the tide gates to be closed during high tides, keeping the Lake level constant at 1.0 feet.

The County operated flood control station is located on the estuary channel at 7th Street. Almost all flood control is done by preventing high tides from entering the Lake, but four diesel operated pumps are also available to prevent flooding.

Plant Growth: Shoreline algae may make a brief appearance in September, but will be essentially gone by October, a victim of cooling water temperatures and decreased daylight. Widgeon grass is but a memory, and when the first fresh water runoff reaches the Lake (carrying a load of nutrients with it) plankton responds with a big bloom, typically turning the Lake a copper, bronze color for several days or until the high tides are allowed to flow back in and restore higher salinity. As plankton blooms reassert their hold on the Lake, the water loses its clarity, becoming murky.

During this time of the year, plankton growth is more noticeable in the upper arms of the Lake, closer to the storm drain / creek outfalls. At times the water behind the black and yellow trash barriers will be pea soup green, while immediately outside the barrier visibility will be 2 - 3 feet.

Urban Runoff: Storm drain flows increase only gradually in early autumn as thirsty soil soaks up the first rains. It is not until the soil becomes saturated by several inches of rain that runoff dramatically increases. With the first storm drain flows come the lightest, most easily floatable street debris, especially ubiquitous pieces of Styrofoam packing material and balls. Plastic bottles and cigarette butts are also commonly found in the first flush of the season.

With the first rains of autumn, hundreds of balls are washed down through storm drains and into Lake Merritt.

Shown here are a small number of them collected in a few months during the fall of 2001.

There have been no measurements of the volume of flow that enters Lake Merritt on a monthly or seasonal basis. This could be accomplished but governments typically do not have hydrologists on staff, and there are no stream gauges or other flow monitoring devices in the creeks and storm drains leading to Lake Merritt. *(Note: A stream gauge was installed in Glen Echo creek).*

Water Quality: Diminishing is the word for water quality as the season progresses. When several tenths of an inch of rain fall, runoff forms a layer of fresh water over the heavier, salty water. Stratification occurs. The bottom layer becomes isolated from the surface, which is being oxygenated by photosynthesis from plankton. To make matters worse, storm drain flows carry in large quantities of material that use up oxygen. These materials settle into the mud at the bottom and continually deplete oxygen from the lower layer of water. Cut off from surface, the bottom layer reaches critically oxygen low levels, often as low as 2 milligrams per liter, and sometimes even less.

Because of low oxygen levels in the bottom layer, the U. S. Environmental Protection Agency has listed Lake Merritt on its 303(d) list as an impaired body of water. The Lake is also listed as impaired due to trash.

Leaves clogging an uncleaned storm drain inlet can move in mass quantities into Lake Merritt in the fall. After sinking to the bottom, they decay, using up oxygen from the bottom layer of Lake water. Citizens are encouraged to adopt a storm drain inlet and keep it clean.

Biological Activity: Decreasing light and temperature trigger changes in life at the Lake as the summer terns depart. They are replaced by cormorants, coots, and later a myriad of ducks from the northern latitudes. As the season progresses, the number of birds increases. At least 100 and up to 400 coots have been counted at the Lake in the fall. Several scaup, ruddy ducks, canvasbacks and goldeneyes can be found by the end of November, but most of them arrive in December.

Many of the migratory birds are born in the Canadian wilderness, fly several days non-stop, and arrive at our urban estuary in the dark of night. Then, when the sun rises, they are greeted by buildings, cars, and people; things they have never seen before. No wonder they are afraid of us!

Cormorant numbers are limited to a small, breeding population at the Lake during the summer, but build up to hundreds or thousands in the fall. They are often seen "herding" schools of fish into the shallow waters where they dive and feast on topsmelt, sculpin and other fish.

Underwater, a different pattern emerges. As algae gives way to plankton, fish and some invertebrates depart the shallow waters for deeper areas, or leave the Lake completely. This trend accelerates as rainfall increases. Others, such as salmon and steelhead begin to move upstream from the ocean and bay toward fresh water spawning grounds. It is not positively known that steelhead trout (which is type of rainbow trout which migrates to the sea and returns several times to fresh water to spawn) passed through Lake Merritt on their way upstream, but is it is very likely they did. Unlike salmon, which require a larger watershed and river, steelhead can colonize smaller streams, and probably utilized the lower portions of Glen Echo creek before most of it was converted into storm drains. Juvenile rainbow trout have been found in Glen Echo creek, perhaps he ancestors of steelhead.

An occasional salmon is still found in Lake Merritt, but they are probably stray fish that became lost trying to find the stream in which they were born. Steelhead are also seen in the Lake during the fall. Some may be fish released into the Lake from hatcheries in the late 1990's as part of the "Fishing in the City" program, but some have intact adipose fins, indicating they may be of wild origin. These wild fish have been found at the mouth of Glen Echo creek, and may spawned, or tried to spawn, in the Richmond Park area.

For some invertebrates, autumn is also a time to spawn. These include the sea slug, a member of the snail family, but which doesn't have a shell. In October of 2001, almost the entire shoreline was coated with the yellow, gelatinous egg masses of this creature. Most people probably never noticed this phenomenon, and others probably considered it to be another form of pollution. But it is just one more example of the myriad of life that the Lake supports.

Millions of sea slug egg masses were found in the Lake in October, 2001.

WINTER (December - February)

Summary: Urban runoff dominates the Lake in winter as rainfall washes trash and chemicals down from the streets. This litter is often visible where it concentrates along the shoreline and behind storm drain barriers. Water clarity is typically low and the Lake level is often kept down to provide capacity for potential floods. Dead animals are relatively common as the water stratifies into layers and the bottom layer losses oxygen. Odors occur when oxygen levels in the bottom layer reach near zero. After heavy rainstorms you may even observe duckweed in the Lake carried down from ponds upstream on Glen Echo creek. But you will not see algae or widgeon grass which grow mainly in the spring and summer. Migratory waterfowl are abundant, attracting many bird enthusiasts from around the Bay Area.

Rainfall washes urban run-off from 4,650 acres into Lake Merritt.

Rainfall averages about 3 - 4 inches per month in the winter, and typically occurs on ten days per month, scouring the watershed and creeks. When El Nino conditions exist, as much as ten inches of precipitation or more may wash into the Lake. Heavy rainfall creates high water and fast flows in the creeks, mobilizing debris that normally does not move (including the television set we once found). Creek banks are purged, washing away brambles, branches, and tree limbs.

Although enormous volumes of fresh water pour into the Lake, there is no data on creek flows. This information would be very useful for both creek management and improving water quality in the Lake. Stream flow gauges are needed.

Flood Control: Because of frequent rainfall, the Lake is very often kept in a flood control mode, held at an elevation of 1.0 feet. This is accomplished by keeping high tides out of the Lake, which is done whenever there is a 50% chance of rain in the forecast. Twice weekly weather forecasts are used by the Alameda County Flood Control District to decide if the tide gates should be kept closed during high tides. Typically, the Lake is kept at a level of 1.0 feet for the duration of the forecast, or until the county crew can get back to the flood control station and re-set the controls. Water entering the Lake from rainfall is allowed to drain out to the Bay, but salt water inflow at high tides is often greatly reduced.

(Note: Different data is now used to determine gate closure. Tide gate controls can now be set remotely).

<u>Plant Growth</u>: Plankton dominates Lake Merritt during the winter, making the water appear murky. For several days after each rain the Lake takes on a bronze color due to a bloom stimulated by fresh water and nutrients washed in from the watershed. Algae and widgeon grass are typically not found due to cold temperatures and short day length.

<u>Urban Runoff</u>: An average of 5,244 pounds of trash per month was removed from Lake Merritt during January of 1998, 1999, 2000 and 2001. Plastic bags, Styrofoam, leaves, paper, bottles, cans, cigarette butts and woody debris from creeks may be found floating, or on the Lake bottom. Where contained by barriers at storm drain outfalls, trash concentrates in impressive quantities. The longer the duration between rainstorms, the more trash accumulates in the watershed to be washed downstream. More intense storms wash in larger quantities of trash.

Storm drain flows carry enormous quantities of urban runoff from the watershed into Lake Merritt. Sixty storm drain outfalls enter the Lake, ranging in size from 12 inches to 6 feet across. They drain a watershed of 4,650 acres, which is 33 times the size of the Lake. Most trash comes from shopping areas and fast food restaurants.

<u>Water Quality</u> reaches its worst due to runoff and fecal matter from increased waterfowl populations. Fecal coliform concentrations rise above the levels not safe for body contact. Visibility is typically only a few feet, especially in the arms of the Lake near large storm drain outfalls. Salinity is highly variable, approaching that of fresh water after big storms, and often half that of sea water when high tide flows are allowed to enter the Lake. Stratification occurs as the lighter, fresh water runoff remains at the surface, trapping the denser, saltier water at the bottom.

But it is dissolved oxygen that presents the worst problem during the winter. When the Lake stratifies into separate surface and bottom layers, the bottom layer often becomes extremely low in oxygen. Readings in the arms of the Lake are frequently below 3 parts per million and have occasionally been measured at 0 - 1. These areas of low oxygen near the bottom often extend to the center area of the lake.

Biological activity is at a minimum when New Year's Day dawns cold and dim. Temperature, daylight, and aquatic life are at a low ebb as the Lake's waters can drop as low as 43° and darkness lasts for 14 hours or more. Nutrients washed in as leaves from storm drains build up in the sediments, ready for the spring bloom. Migratory waterfowl are the main attraction at the Lake in the winter as their numbers increase to over 1,000 birds. Coots, scaup and goldeneye ducks are the most common winter migrants. Several hundred of them are counted every winter, and smaller numbers of ruddy ducks, canvasbacks, widgeon, and pintails may also be found.

Lake Merritt is a refuge for hundreds of migratory birds in the winter. To minimize their disturbance, boat access to the Trestle Glen arm of the Lake is prohibited from November 1 to May 1. Protection of game birds and wild animals at the Lake began in 1870 after passage of a state law.

Under the surface, aquatic life struggles to survive poor water quality, or moves out of the Lake into the Bay. Animals that can't leave the Lake (like mussels and barnacles and shrimp) or animals which are too large to pass through the 7.5 inch wide bars at the flood control station, typically die. Death occurs in many ways: Death by low oxygen; death by starvation; death by chemical pollution; by ingesting trash in the false hope that it is food; by cold temperatures; and death by a marine, tidal lagoon suddenly turning into fresh water. Life becomes hard, and by winter's end, populations are at an annual low. Large bat rays, salmonid fish and striped bass are sometimes found dead during the winter at Lake Merritt. Myriads of small fish survive however, and provide food for winter waterfowl.

Improvement to low oxygen levels in the bottom layer could be achieved by re-designing the flood control station to draw water from the bottom of the Lake, rather than the top.

EPILOGUE

Lake Merritt is not a Lake, but a tidal lagoon. Although it has been modified by the hand of man for over 150 years, it is in many ways still part of the natural world. The open space, relative quiet and serenity stand in sharp contrast to the highways, high rises and high profiles of streets and buildings that surround its waters. To the extent that it retains these natural qualities is a testament in part to the resilience of life, and also to the people who have helped to preserve them.

Lake Merritt is many things to many people; the jewel of Oakland to some, a wildlife refuge to others; a big smelly pond to a few, and a jogging path to many. It is the view out their window to tens of thousands of people, and the peace that calms their soul. On a more practical note, it is a climate buffer, moderating the extremes of temperature in the city. Hydrologists look upon it as a flood control basin and boaters as a recreational resource.

As the first years of the new century begin to pass by, efforts to restore this "urban estuary" are gathering force. Plans are being developed to re-establish a small wetland along its shores. A master plan has been written and brave, new proposals have been created to restore part of the natural tidal flows that once carried large ships to its banks. To the extent they are successful, these efforts will enhance the Lake, as well as property values around it.

Through it all, the seasons continue; ever changing, ever reminding us of our relationship to the Lake. For 10,000 years the creeks and tidal waters have flowed here. For the next 10,000 they may continue their cycles, provided we understand what we have been given, what we have created, and how they can work together.

(Note: in later years, $198,250,000 from Measure DD bonds (passed in 2002), funded extensive capital improvements to Lakeside Park, and improved tidal circulation).

PHOTOS BY JOHN KIRKMIRE

To view these and more beautiful photos of Lake Merritt, visit
https://www.nowandlens.com/

EPILOGUE

History is repeating itself. Water quality problems are simmering, and a newly formed Lake Merritt Conservancy is fighting to improve not just the water, but also Lakeside Park, and the image of Oakland as well. As these past essays tell us, the process is long and hard, but the results are worth it.

Despite some progress, the 1990's still haunt us. The relevance of issues from the 1990's to today is obvious. Fish kills (similar to those in the past), plankton blooms, nuisance algae, and a shortage of wildlife habitat continue to plague Lake Merritt.

Recurrent periods of very low oxygen still oc-cur in several places, and in 2022, a massive fish kill occurred. On August 28 of that year, oxygen levels of zero were measured at both the surface and bottom throughout the water column (an event never before witnessed at the lake). Levels of zero to two continued for six days. During those days, an enormous fish kill enveloped the lake, resulting in tens of thousands of dead fish, as well as numerous clams, mussels, shrimp, etc. These prob-lems not only looked bad, they also smelled bad.

Because conditions have not changed, the threat of another deadly plankton bloom looms just beyond the horizon.

On a broader scale, budget problems, staff shortages, homeless issues, those who choose to litter, and apathy are still with us today.

Summary: Since the last of these essays were written, there has been a lot of water under the bridge at the channel. Trash from urban runoff, especially plastic pollution, has declined, yet low oxygen problems re-main. Measure DD bond improvements have enhanced infrastructure, but funds have become exhausted and maintenance is difficult.

Wintering waterfowl continue their seasonal residence, yet habitat improvement remains elusive and the Nature Center is only open part time. Lake Merritt Institute volunteers still work valiantly to keep the Lake clean, but homeless encampments, graffiti, vandalism, arson, and illegal littering continue to degrade the park. Thousands of people jog, walk and rest in Lakeside Park, but a few ignore park rules, which are often unenforced. City government provides basic services, but budget limitations and staff shortages hinder efforts to let the Lake reach its potential.

Following are some the recent efforts to maintain and enhance Lake Merritt and Lakeside Park.

Lake Merritt Water Quality Management Pilot Project: Phase One: 2023 - 2025

 In response to the massive fish kill of 2022, the City of Oakland implemented the Lake Merritt Water Quality Management Pilot Project, one of a long series of management plans aimed at our downtown estuary. Working with partners, this program monitors water quality, seeks to prevent future fish kills, and maintain healthy conditions for wildlife. It is designed to address excessive algae growth and low dissolved oxygen levels associated with the fish kill.

https://www.oaklandca.gov/topics/lake-merritt-water-quality-management-pilot-project

The first phase of the Pilot is underway and includes: Continuous monitoring of dissolved oxygen and other water quality parameters at Lake Merritt, limited stakeholder engagement, a review of prior water quality data collected by others at Lake Merritt, and the installation of two devices to increase dissolved oxygen. The first of these devices, a low aeration fountain, was installed August 15, 2023 near the Pergola by El Embarcadero Avenue and replaces an out-of-service fountain at that location. By mixing air into the water, the fountain will improve dissolved oxygen (DO) levels in the Lake, helping to maintain an oxygenated refuge for aquatic life near the fountain. The design and spray settings on the new fountain maximize benefit to wildlife.

An oxygenation device was installed September 27, 2023 and was fully operational October 16, 2023, in the area near where Glen Echo Creek enters the Lake. This device pumps micro bubble oxygen into the water at the Lake bottom. The results of the first phase will inform the scope and need for subsequent work. Oakland's Capital Improvement Program lists this work as unfunded under the "Lake Merritt Water Quality Management Plan Development and Implementation - Healthy Lake Initiative." This work will proceed as funding becomes available in future budget cycles and/or through grants. Success at Lake Merritt will borrow from and inform approaches at other water bodies, threats becoming more common with climate change."

The City of Oakland recently received a one million dollar grant to assist in the effort.

A TMDL is Being Planned

Total maximum daily load (TMDL) is an acronym used in water quality regulations. It refers to the maximum amount of a pollutant that can be allowed, but is also used to mean any planning process to improve water quality. These long term governmental actions are sometimes begun when a body of water is formally listed as impaired and threatened, and placed on a list under provisions of section 303(d) of the federal Clean Water Act. In 1999, Lake Merritt was so listed due to trash, organic enrichment, and low oxygen. Agencies responsible for waters so listed are required by the Clean Water Act to take actions for removal from the list. Legal action for failure to do so is possible.

A series of stakeholder meetings are planned under the auspices of the San Francisco Regional Water Quality Control Board. Possible actions to remove Lake Merritt from the 303(d) list could include: Removal of sediment by dredging; installation of multiple oxygen machines and/or surface aerators, continuous water quality monitoring expanded to include benthos and plankton, resumption of meetings by the multi-agency Water Quality Technical Committee, reducing nutrient input from the watershed, chemical treatment of the sediment, additional storm drain filters, possible enhancements to the flood control station, and other actions deemed appropriate. Many of these projects were mentioned in these essays.

As part of the TMDL process, a website will be established, and a Technical Advisory Committee will be convened. Data synthesis will occur in 2026, and a final report prepared in 2028.

Lake Merritt Commons

Access hourly water quality data at three locations from the LakeTech, Inc. platform at "Lake Merritt Commons" on Facebook. https://www.facebook.com/profile.php?id=61554247913101

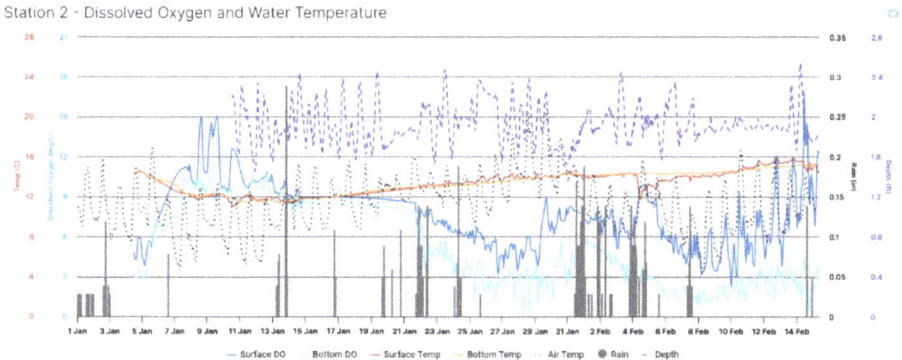

Station 2 - Dissolved Oxygen and Water Temperature

Cultural diversity remains Oakland's strength: The wonderful diversity of Oakland continues to expand, encompassing more people while embracing new traditions, flavors, and colors. Today, musical drumming, lovers holding hands,

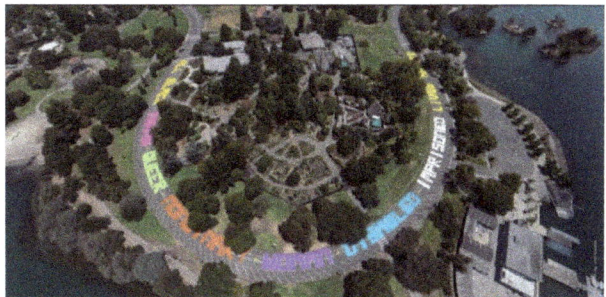

and unexpected art are frequent sights by the waters. Lake Merritt, never judgmental, continues to welcome all to her shores. Shown here is Diversity Road in Lakeside Park.

As mentioned in essay 51, everyone can enjoy its beauty. The welcoming of people of all races, religions, genders, languages, and values continues.

A balance must be found

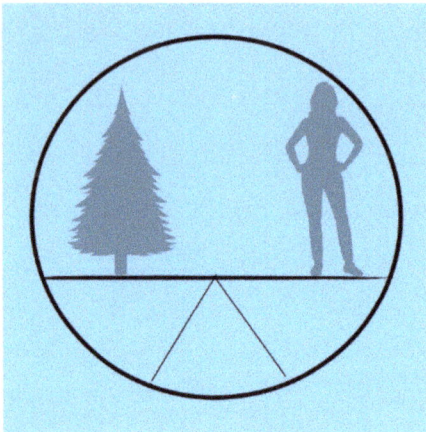

In 1969, at the dawn of the first Earth Day, a new symbol of the environmental movement emerged. It was called the Balance Button, and featured a tree representing nature, and a stick figure representing civilization on each end of a see saw. Tip the teeter totter one way with the tree up, and the environment would be over emphasized. Tip it the other way and civilization would be out of balance with nature.

This balance applies not only to civilization and nature, but also to poverty and wealth, stewardship and apathy, and respect and dismissal.

New concerns challenge us.

Homelessness, increased crime, vandalism and even arson threaten the ability of the city to manage the Lake. These things peck away at the value of Lakeside Park, scare away children and lower civic pride. They also lower real estate values, chase away businesses, and degrade political fortunes. Some issues have been solved, some are being worked on, but too many remain.

Enduring climate change and accompanying sea level rise threaten the long term future of Lakeside Park. Such low lying areas are particularly vulnerable to flooding, and the existing Alameda County flood control and pump station located along the channel can only provide protection from the 25 year storm. As sea level rise increases, this protection will diminish. A redesigned flood control station could provide:

- Protection from the 100+ year flood. Larger pumps and perhaps larger inlet / outlet channels could accomplish this.

- A channel for boat access between the lake and Oakland Inner Harbor. This was part of the original Measure DD bond projects, but had to be sidelined. This channel would be closed off if needed during flood conditions.

- Creation of a new Water Board permit for the new structure, which would bring the county under controls that would fine tune operation of the new station to optimally balance water quality and flood control. For example, what is the actual cost of an 1-2 percent increase in flooding vs. tide gate operation that would prevent a plankton bloom and fish kill?

- Opportunities for obtaining a grant from existing sea level rise programs.

What's Next?

We can reflect on several generations of how people have interacted with the waters we now call lake Merritt: Exploitation, expansion, development, pollution, recognition, improvement, and appreciation. As the post covid era dawns, one thing is certain. The lake will be here; how shall we relate to it? Join the above mentioned efforts and become an activist: Your efforts will be rewarded.

ESSAY 78. LAKE MERRITT: THE JOURNEY CONTINUES

By Jonathan Hoffberg

Spring, 2024

The Lake Merritt Conservancy Coalition

Residents, volunteers, and businesspeople of Lake Merritt and the surrounds have been gathering in small groups of 20-30 people around the lake to ask ourselves how we might join forces to create a better experience for all Lake stakeholders. Many of us have lived in the lake district for many years, and have seen the lake's ups and downs. We know what it can be like, and we also recognize the lake, the park, and the community, are all operating under some form of duress.

The Lake Merritt Master Plan, adopted in 2002, made the case for the establishment of a Conservancy to realize and act as a steward for the plan and keep it up to date. As we face new challenges and community needs, and as the Clean Water/Safe Parks (Measure DD) funds draw to a close, we recognize that the LMMP is ready for an update, and that update should be done in an intentional and equitable way.

Given the City's budget deficit, we recognize that other sources of financing will be needed to make this happen. A non-profit Conservancy, working in partnership with the City, can raise money for capital improvements and all manner of environmental design elements, and gain access to funds that may not be available to the City government. We can also work on procuring public funds in concert with the City in a way that can supplement the City's grant application process.

We are coming together in an intentional and organized way to ask ourselves:
"How May We...Build a Conservancy, a non-profit organization whose intention is to act in a Public-Private Partnership with the City of Oakland, as a steward of the lake and the parkland around it, to revitalize our park and meaningfully address issues of ecology, pollution, crime, homelessness and social equity so that the lake stands as a beacon to communities everywhere, for our children, our children's children, and many generations beyond...."

We are workshopping questions around Equity, Outreach, Governance, Safety, Environmental Design, Ecology, and the Park Experience, and we're beginning the process of assembling the output of those workshops into a draft vision… a working document where we explore the World of the Possible.

In partnership with other non-profit organizations, civic and business leaders in the community, we are investigating ways in which we can harness local resources to create new triple-bottom-line businesses that solve problems for the lake community, and in so doing, create an economic engine that will fund the Conservancy in perpetuity.

What is a Conservancy?

Conservancies are private, non-profit park organizations that raise money independent of the city and spend it under a plan of action mutually agreed upon with the government.

Conservancies have emerged in the last few decades as viable complements to traditional city governance in hundreds of city parks and public spaces around the country.

A Lake Merritt Conservancy could benefit and amplify the work of all these volunteer organizations, an impressive list!

Adams Point Neighborhood Group. Alameda County Master Gardeners. Autumn Lights Festival. Bonsai Gardens. California Center for Natural History. Camron-Stanford House. Children's Fairyland. Cleveland Cascades. Community for Lake Merritt. East Bay Front Runners & Walkers. Essex Community Action Committee. Friends of the Gardens at Lake Merritt. Junior Center of Art & Science. Friends of the Oakland Municipal Band. Lake Merritt Advocates. Lake Merritt Breakfast Club. Lake Merritt Community Alliance. Lake Merritt Institute. Lake Merritt Joggers & Striders. Lake Merritt Rowing Club. Lake Merritt Weed Warriors. Lakeshore Neighbors. Measure DD Community Coalition. Oakland Croquet Club. Oakland East Bay Garden Center. Oakland Lawn Bowling Club. Oakland Museum of California. Oakland Parks and recreation Foundation. Oakland Public Works Adopt-a-Spot. Oakland

Where Have Conservancies Succeeded?

- New York City's Central Park Conservancy, established in 1980, was one of the first and has become a model.
- The Piedmont Conservancy in Atlanta is an example of a conservancy on a scale more similar to our own.
- Nationally, parkland under the purview of the conservancies is almost 35,000 acres and growing.

The Problem

Our lake is out of balance. The unhoused make their homes here, endangering themselves and the larger community. Untended trash sets an example. Neglect becomes the norm, paid for by local wildlife, while a deafening chorus of urban escapism on park property further undercuts the quality of life for lakeside residents and wildlife.

Current Solutions

The City's Department of Public Works, with its 78 square miles of urban landscape to attend, and an endless backlog of urban decay, is spread way too thin to properly maintain water quality and lake's perimeter, the edge of a tidal lagoon that's home to the United States' oldest designated wildlife refuge. Lake Merritt has a robust volunteer community that does its best to fill the gap between what the city can provide and what the community needs.

Benefits of a Lake Merritt Conservancy

- Improved Standard of Care for the lake
- A (More) United Voice at City Hall
- Economies of Scale for Volunteer Efforts
- Coordination Across All Lake Caretakers
- New Opportunities for Oakland Residents

A robust volunteer community

To learn more, go to: https://www.lakemc.org/home

CITATIONS TO PREVIOUS MANAGEMENT PLANS AND STUDIES, ETC.

Lake Merrit Flood Control. Brown & Caldwell Engineers. Prepared for the Alameda County Flood Control District. 1966.

Lake Management Plan Report, Phase 1. 1977. Woodward Clyde Consultants, San Francisco, CA. 22 pages. May, 1977.

Lake Merrit Biological and Water Quality Data. Biological Sciences Department. Merritt College. 1977.

Lake Merritt Restoration Project, Final Report. CH2M Hill, Jefferson and Associates and Gary Shawley. Alameda County Flood Control & Water Conservation District. Submitted to: U.S. Environmental Protection Agency Region IX and California Water Resources Control Board. 128 pages. January, 1982.

Lake Merritt Management Plan. City of Oakland. 31 pages. June, 1987.

Lake Merritt Park, Recommendations for a Master Plan. American Society of Landscape Architects. The Community Assistance Team (CAT) study. 1989.

Final Report on Lake Management. Lake Merritt Estuary. Alameda County Flood Control and Water Conservation District. Engineering Science. February, 1990.

Final Report on Lake Management. Lake Merritt Estuary. Alameda County Flood Control and Water Conservation District. Engineering Science. March, 1991.

Final Report on Lake Management. Lake Merritt Estuary. Alameda County Flood Control and Water Conservation District. Engineering Science. January, 1992.

Lake Merritt: The Resource Enhancement Plan; Water Quality Study. Final Report. 1992. Water Quality Associates. Prepared for: The City of Oakland Office of Parks and Recreation and Office of Public Works. September, 1992.

Lake Merritt: The Resource Enhancement Plan; Water Quality Study. Appendices. Water Quality Associates. Prepared for: The City of Oakland Office of Parks and Recreation and Office of Public Works. September, 1992.

Lake Merritt Siltation Study. Water Quality Associates. Prepared for the City of Oakland. 1992.

Final Report on Lake Management. Lake Merritt Estuary. Alameda County Flood Control and Water Conservation District. Prepared by Engineering Science. February, 1993.

Pond of Dreams; Lake Merritt History. The EXPRESS, 17:7. Oakland, CA. Glen David Gold. November, 25, 1994.

Final Report on Lake Management.   Lake Merritt Estuary.   Alameda County Flood Control and Water Conservation District. Engineering Science. February, 1994.

Lake Merritt Sediment Investigation. Moju Environmental. Prepared for the City of Oakland. 1994.

Final Report on Lake Management.   Lake Merritt Estuary.   Alameda County Flood Control and Water Conservation District. Engineering Science. February, 1995.

A Historical and Environmental Geographic Analysis of Lake Merritt. M.A. Thesis. San Francisco State University. Mary A. Travis. 1995.

Water Quality Monitoring Report. Lake Merritt Estuary.   Alameda County Public Works Agency. October, 1996.

White Paper on Water Level Control and Tidal Flows. The Lake Merritt Institute. 10 pages. Updated, October, 2002.

Lake Merritt Water Quality Monitoring Report – September 2005 to September 2006. Geomatrix Consultants, Inc. 9 pages. January, 2007.

2014 Lake Merritt Institute website prior to the loss of data. https://web.archive.org/web/20140526002040/http://www.lakemerritt-institute.org/

Gondola Cruises on Lake Merritt   https://www.dolcevitagondola.com/

ABOUT THE AUTHOR

Richard L. Bailey holds degrees in zoology and a Ph.D. in forest resources. He has traveled extensively and worked in state and federal government sectors, for consulting firms, and in private industry. He is the author of "Stormy: A novel of Climate Change."

He founded the Lake Merritt Institute and served as its executive director until 2015, writing many issues of "Tidings" (an Institute newsletter) giving educational presentations, and coordinating volunteer efforts to remove trash from the Lake.

He currently lives Novato with his wife Susan, golden retriever Finnegan, and a mated pair of angelfish.

www.ingramcontent.com/pod-product-compliance
Lightning Source LLC
Chambersburg PA
CBHW051245020426

42333CB00025B/3057